Lost My Partner — What'll I Do?

A Clear, Practical Guide
For Coping and Finding Strength
When Your Spouse Dies

LAURIE J. SPECTOR, M.S.W.
and
RUTH SPECTOR WEBSTER, M.S.W.

M[illegible]
Manhattan Beach, California

LOST MY PARTNER - WHAT'LL I DO?

Published by McCormick Press
Library of Congress Catalogue Card Number 99-93080
ISBN: 0-9668262-0-5

FIRST EDITION

Cover design by Robert Aulicino
Layout design by Rosalie Carlson

10 9 8 7 6 5 4 3 2 1

Dedication

In memory of Donald E. Spector, Ph.D.,
whose love and courage was the inspiration
for this book.

Contents

PART THREE / MOVING ON

PART FOUR / HELP ALONG THE WAY

About The Authors

Laurie J. Spector, M.S.W., and Ruth Spector Webster, M.S.W., have the advantage of being daughter and mother as well as psychotherapists experienced in counseling the bereaved. Their personal relationship affords them added insight into the experience of loss within a family as well as invaluable perspectives on the particular concerns of different generations.

Laurie J. Spector graduated from the University of California at Los Angeles with a Masters' Degree in Social Work. She has worked as a psychotherapist in both medical and psychiatric settings, and has done in-home counseling of cancer patients and their families. She developed and conducted bereavement groups for a home health agency as well as a support group for medical staff. The popularity of her holiday season bereavement groups led her to develop and conduct a presentation that specifically focuses on coping with loss at this difficult time of year. She has also lectured to other psychotherapists on how to counsel the bereaved. Ms. Spector lives with her husband in Manhattan Beach, California, where she maintains a private practice.

Ruth Spector Webster was herself widowed while in her midforties, and her unique understanding is reflected in the "having been there" feeling of *LOST MY PARTNER*. Her own loss profoundly shaped the direction of her professional work. After obtaining her Masters' Degree in

Social Work at the University of Southern California, Ms. Webster went on to develop and conduct widowed groups as a psychotherapist in the Department of Psychiatry at Kaiser Permanente in Woodland Hills, California. In addition to her group work, she has counseled individuals and families as well as conducted inservice presentations for other professionals on spousal loss. She has lectured to seniors and various community groups on how to cope with the death of a spouse. Ms. Webster is remarried and currently lives in Malibu, California.

Acknowledgements

Rosalyn Benitez-Bloch, D.S.W., deserves our special thanks for the time, expertise, and encouragement she graciously provided through several rewrites of this book.

The comments and enthusiastic responses of Eve Marsh, Anita Fresco, and William Hinkson in the months following their own losses provided an invaluable confirmation of our vision for this book.

Our deepest appreciation to Laurie's husband, Michael Hassul, Ph.D, for his patience, guidance, assistance, and unflagging support in helping launch this publication.

We're very grateful for the generosity of Ann Berger's editorial expertise in preparing the final manuscript.

We thank Holly Hodder, Editor at Freeman Press, for her encouraging efforts on our behalf during the early phases of the writing.

For her knowledgeable services as editor and referee in the final stages of this book, we thank Vivian M. Barnert, M.S.W.

We thank Evelyn Tabachnick, Ph.D, for helping us better understand the impact of parental loss on children and adolescents.

Martin S. Roden, Donald Kunitz, and Lee Ona Hostrop have been generous in offering information, advice, and encouragement about self-publishing.

The thoughtful criticism and suggestions by members of the South Bay Writer's Club throughout the rewriting process have been invaluable.

Ruth is particularly indebted to L. Jeannette Davis, D.S.W., for guiding her both before and after Don's death and helping her understand that one can grow from the experience of bereavement.

Our love and appreciation to Bob Webster, Andrea Spector, and all our family and friends for the many ways they've been there for us throughout the progress of this book.

Finally, the book would not have been possible without the many people who have, over the years, shared with us the pain and triumphs of their own bereavement experiences.

Before You Start This Book

Few of life's changes are as turbulent as the death of a spouse.

Unlike other losses, it is a time when almost everything in your life changes.

LOST MY PARTNER will take you from the first painful months following the death to the time when you'll feel able to truly "move on" in a way that feels right for you. We've distilled important clinical information into a condensed easy-to-read format. From our years of counseling the widowed, we've selected the most proven and effective suggestions and coping techniques. We've made the book itself so easy to use that you can turn to it at work or at home whenever you need advice or the pain of your loss feels especially intense and/or unpredictable.

Whether you're a man or woman, young or old, we encourage you to be gentle and patient with yourself and to use this book in whatever way is most helpful: either read it all the way through or pick and choose only those chapters that feel most relevant at the time.

You may find that it's just too soon and you don't feel ready to continue on with *LOST MY PARTNER*. That's OK. No matter how much advice and guidance is offered, you will grieve in *your own way* and in *your own time.*

Having made my way through my own pain, I know how overwhelming the journey can look at the beginning.

I remember sitting beside my husband shortly after he'd been diagnosed with terminal cancer and trying to imagine what it would be like to lose him. How will it feel, I wondered, to wake up without Don beside me? What about all the thoughts and moments, both small and important, I'd grown accustomed to sharing with this man for the past twenty-five years? How would I possibly cope without him?

Having married young, Don and I had literally grown up together. We'd raised three children, Don had left a family business to become a clinical psychologist, and now, because of his encouragement and support, I was about to embark on a new career of my own.

When Don died fourteen months later, however, I realized that nothing I'd imagined during his illness could have prepared me for the reality of actually losing him.

There were many times when I felt like my entire world was turned upside down. The pain was so intense, I wondered if it would ever soften. Would I ever enjoy all the small things that I once took for granted? Would food ever taste good again? Could I ever see myself as a "single person," much less pursue other relationships? I felt my grief would continue in this same way forever.

It didn't. In moments of despair, I learned to remind myself to look back and see how far I'd already progressed.

As I struggled to understand what was happening, it slowly dawned on me that I had one of two choices: I could either remain right where I was for the rest of my life or I could go forward. My future was in my own hands.

I made the choice to go forward. It wasn't easy. The grieving process was difficult; there were no shortcuts. As time went on, however, I discovered that the pain did get easier, food began to taste good again, and the small pleasures of life returned.

I went on to a career as a clinical social worker, where I soon discovered that my experience of loss gave me a new depth of understanding not found in textbooks on bereavement. As I conducted support groups and counseled the widowed, I found that this added another dimension to my work. When asked by patients, colleagues, or physicians to recommend a book on the subject, I was frustrated. All the existing publications I found were either too wordy, overly clinical, or didn't relate to what I or my patients had actually gone through.

My daughter Laurie also chose a career in clinical social work, where, as a part of her private practice, she too conducted bereavement groups. One day she suggested we combine our years of personal and clinical experience to create a book on spousal loss specifically written with the grieving reader in mind.

Within the pages of this book, you'll find chapters organized into four sections: WHAT'S GOING ON?, GETTING THROUGH THE DAYS, MOVING ON, and HELP ALONG THE WAY.

WHAT'S GOING ON? focuses on understanding the various emotional and physical symptoms of bereavement. It offers techniques for coping with these symptoms.

GETTING THROUGH THE DAYS takes you through many of the most common situations you may have to deal with: the effect of the loss on your children; coping with other family members, friends, and coworkers; spiritual concerns; financial headaches; disposing of your spouse's belongings, and surviving the holidays.

MOVING ON deals with coming to terms with a changing identity and discovering ways to create new friends and find companionship.

HELP ALONG THE WAY includes a list of our most important tips that you can carry with you as well as a section filled with resources for everything from grief counselling to volunteer and social opportunities.

However you choose to use *LOST MY PARTNER*, Laurie and I believe it will make your bereavement easier.

Ruth Spector Webster

Part One

What's Going On?

CHAPTER ONE

Not Normal Is Normal

You look in the mirror and say to yourself:

"I look like me but I don't feel like me. Everything in my life seems to be changing. I'm not reacting the way I usually do. What's happening? Am I going crazy?"

NO, YOU AREN'T. You're going through one of the most intense, frightening and difficult emotional experiences of life: bereavement.

Your whole world has been turned upside down. You may have experienced other losses, but losing a spouse affects everything in your life. Both your mind and body are struggling to come to terms with the loss. Realistically, you can't expect to be your normal self.

Try not to compare how you're coping and progressing with anyone else; each person is unique in how he or she moves through bereavement.

Almost everyone, however, experiences some of the following reactions:

- DIFFICULTY CONCENTRATING

  "It takes so much energy to focus on what I once did so easily. I can't read a newspaper or follow a TV program as I used to."

- SLEEP DISTURBANCES

  "I fall asleep; and 2 hours later, I'm wide awake." or *"I'm exhausted, but I toss and turn for hours,"* or *"I just want to sleep all the time."*

- APPETITE DISTURBANCES

  " Nothing tastes good anymore." or *"Food is the only thing that feels good."*

- LACK OF ENERGY/HYPERACTIVITY

  "I feel so exhausted all the time, even though I haven't done anything." or *"I feel so restless—I can't sit still."*

- PREOCCUPATION WITH THE LOSS

  "From the moment I open my eyes in the morning, it seems that I can't stop thinking about what's happened."

- INCREASED ANXIETY OR WORRY

  "What's going to happen to me? How will I ever manage without my spouse?" or *"Do I have enough money to live on, and will I know how to handle it?"*

- *NUMBNESS AND/OR A SENSE OF UNREALITY*

  "I'm like a robot who's just going through the motions. I feel that I'm watching myself react."

- CRYING SUDDENLY OR FOR NO APPARENT REASON OR AN INABILITY TO CRY

  "I don't know what hit me. I was driving my car, and all of a sudden I burst into tears." or *"I'm afraid once I start crying, I won't be able to stop."* or *"I shouldn't indulge in self-pity when there's really so much to be grateful for."*

- PERSISTENT FEELINGS OF GUILT OR REMORSE

  "If only I'd done more" or *"Why did/didn't I say those things?"*

- ANGER AT THE LOSS/OTHER PEOPLE/GOD

  "Why did this have to happen to me/us?" or *"That doctor/hospital let this happen!"* or *"How could God let this happen?"*

- ABSENTMINDEDNESS

  "I can't seem to remember where I've left things from one minute to the next. It's gotten so bad, I'm afraid I'm getting Alzheimer's."

- SENSE OF RELIEF

  "I feel guilty saying this, but it's a relief to have the nightmare over with."

- SENSE OF LONGING

"When I got back from my trip, I opened the front door and thought she'd be there." or "I saw someone from the back who looked so much like him that for a moment I thought it was my husband."

- DREAMS OR ABSENCE OF DREAMS ABOUT YOUR SPOUSE

"Seeing my husband in a dream was so comforting." or "I wish I could dream about my wife once in a while."

- BODILY SENSATIONS, SUCH AS AN "EMPTY FEELING", FREQUENT SIGHING, OR BEING VERY SENSITIVE TO LOUD NOISES

"Since he died, I feel hollow inside" or "My daughter says I sigh a lot" or "I usually love to be with my little grandchildren, but lately the sound of their high-pitched voices really bothers me."

- SUICIDAL THOUGHTS

"Life is so painful right now that I find myself thinking about ending it, so I can be with my spouse again."

- SENSE OF YOUR SPOUSE'S PRESENCE

"It sounds strange, but there are times when I think I can feel my husband in the room with me."

- TALKING TO YOUR SPOUSE

  "I often find myself talking to my wife as though she were still here." or "I'm so used to discussing important decisions with my husband that I still ask him what to do."

All of these reactions are normal. Some will come and go, while others may continue for awhile. If you feel concerned about any of these feelings, especially suicidal thoughts, talk to a professional counselor, psychotherapist, your doctor, or friends you can trust (See Chapter 7, **Suicidal Thoughts and Other Scary Stuff**).

What's Going On?

CHAPTER TWO

When Will This Be Over?

Bereavement is often described as feeling you are stuck on a rollercoaster. Nobody chooses this ride, but once it starts, you have to hold on tight and trust you'll eventually be back on solid ground. The first few dips can be unsettling, and just when the track straightens out and you think you can finally relax, there may be a few more dips before you get to the finish.

The hopeful news is, if you don't try to jump out before the ride finishes, and if you have someone (or a group) beside you for support, the dips will come less frequently, and you'll recover more quickly.

"How long will this ride take?"

In most cultures of the world, the period of mourning is traditionally one year; however *the answer is different for everyone.*

How long yours lasts depends on:

* Whether your spouse's death was sudden or expected and the circumstances of his/her death. An expected

death generally gives you time to do some anticipatory grieving. A death caused by sudden and/or unusual circumstances will take longer to grieve, because there was no way to prepare for the loss.

* The emotional climate of your relationship with your spouse. Troubled marriages tend to take longer to grieve.

* How you've grieved previous losses in your life.

* The ways you've observed family members mourn, which gives you (rightly or wrongly) a model of "how to grieve." Was it important to appear "strong" and unemotional?

* Whether you've lost anyone else (multiple losses) recently. You may feel overwhelmed by "still another" death.

"When will this be over?"

We can't stress enough the importance of listening to yourself. If you don't try to rush the process or let others pressure you into "snapping out of it", you'll know when the period of acute mourning is over. Most people tell us they know they've reached the end of bereavement when they are:

NO LONGER PREOCCUPIED WITH THEIR LOSS. This doesn't mean they no longer think about or miss their spouse, only that they've found a place inside themselves for that loved one.

READY TO BEGIN MAKING NEW ATTACHMENTS IN THEIR LIVES. This doesn't necessarily mean dating and finding a new spouse, but rather feeling like they can risk closeness to other people again.

ON THE WAY TO CREATING A NEW SENSE OF WHO THEY ARE. You used to be the other half of a couple, and now you aren't. When you marry, you blend yourself into who your spouse is, in order to become a "couple". The length of your marriage and the age at which you married will affect the extent to which your sense of identity is based on being part of that couple.

"Will I ever get used to being on my own?"

Try to remember the time before you had a partner. Think about what you were like and how it felt to do things on your own. Were there qualities within you that once made adapting to changes easier? What dreams and ambitions were set aside because of marriage and its responsibilities? Now that you have the wisdom and experience you lacked at an earlier age, can you see how your abilities have grown and developed with time?

"How can I possibly learn how to handle all those things my spouse used to do?"

Here are important points to keep in mind:

- ▶ FOR NOW, NOT NORMAL IS NORMAL. Give yourself permission to be different in some ways while you're going through bereavement. Try to be patient.

► CRYING IS A HEALTHY EXPRESSION OF YOUR PAIN. Some of you, however, may consider tears a form of "self-pity" and become critical of yourself when you feel the need to cry. Remind yourself that as you go through bereavement, crying *for any reason* is normal and appropriate and Nature's way of releasing emotional tension. If you are having difficulty crying, try the following:

1) Cry in the shower. Sometimes all that water covering you is conducive to shedding tears.

2) Watch a sad movie. This may be more comfortable to do at home.

3) If you fear that you will be unable to stop the tears, set a time limit for your cry. Set a timer for three, five or ten minutes, and when it rings, that is your signal to stop your tears. This may be done on a regular or as-needed basis. You are the best judge of to how to schedule yourself.

4) Listening, looking, and smelling are all sure ways to produce tears. *Listen* to a favorite record or CD that reminds you of your spouse or a recording of his/her voice. *Look* at pictures of your spouse in a video or photo album. *Smell* a favorite item of clothing or cologne.

Remember, tears are a *healthy* expression of your pain and loss, and holding them back will delay the grief process.

- PRIORITIZE. Before you consider any new task, ask yourself how important it really is. Can it wait until you're feeling more up to tackling it?

- NOTICE HOW FAR YOU HAVE COME SINCE THE DEATH. Recall how you were functioning a week, a month, or months ago.

  Many people find that recording their progress in a journal helps them realize how far they've actually come. Writing is also an effective way to come to terms with painful or difficult feelings or events.

- IT'S OKAY TO ASK FOR HELP. Nobody's strong *all* the time. [Even Superman can be weakened by Kryptonite.]

- REMEMBER: YOU HAVE CHOICES. You don't have to do everything your spouse did. It's up to you: do you want to learn how to do something yourself, ask a friend to do it, or hire a professional?

- RECALL THE FIRST TIME YOU TRIED TO DO SOMETHING THAT NOW COMES EASILY. It was probably hard at first, and you made some mistakes. Once you got used to it, though, you became more confident.

CHAPTER THREE

Eating, Sleeping, and Other Necessities of Life

"Sometimes I toss and turn all night. My mind keeps dwelling on what happened."

"I fall asleep, but a few hours later I'm wide awake and can't get back to sleep."

"I wake up much too early. I lie in bed hoping I'll doze off again, but it doesn't work."

With all the changes and stresses you're dealing with, your mind and body are overloaded; it's no wonder you can't rest. Some disturbance in your normal sleep pattern should be expected. The good news is that with time, this disruption goes away on its own. In the meantime, keep in mind that everything seems worse at night. Once morning arrives, the problem that kept you tossing usually appears more manageable.

Here, however, are some practical tips for dealing with that long stretch before the alarm clock goes off:

* BED IS FOR SLEEPING ONLY. Once you're awake, get out of bed and sit in a chair. Read a boring book or watch an uninteresting television show. Return to bed *only* when you begin to feel drowsy.

* DON'T LOOK AT THE CLOCK. Noticing how long it's taking you to fall asleep becomes another pressure.

* IF YOU'RE HAVING PERSISTENT THOUGHTS OR WORRIES, WRITE THEM DOWN. Often writing something down is a way to "get it off your mind." Tell yourself that, like Scarlett O'Hara, "Tomorrow is another day!"

* LISTEN TO THE RADIO AT A LOW VOLUME. Having to strain a bit to hear what's being said forces you to concentrate, so you're diverted from other thoughts or worries.

* LISTEN TO A RELAXATION TAPE. Available at libraries and book stores, these tapes are designed to relax you to the point where you drift into sleep. You may want to remain in bed for this one. Even if you don't use a tape, the following breathing technique will help you relax: take a long, slow breath through your nose, hold it for five seconds, then slowly let it out through your mouth. Repeat the process five times. (If you have a heart condition, check with your doctor before attempting the above.)

* TRY TO GET SOME EXERCISE EARLIER IN THE DAY. For some people, lack of energy while grieving results in their being less physically active during the day. Ask your doctor about some form of mild exercise like walking that can be done earlier in the day to help you sleep at night.

A word on the subject of having something to drink to help you fall asleep: We recommend a glass of warm milk, which will produce the desired chemical reaction in your body. Alcohol, on the other hand, doesn't. While it may at first lift your mood and feel relaxing, alcohol is, in fact, a depressant (which is the last thing you need right now). Alcohol also disrupts your normal sleep cycle, so you aren't getting the quality of rest your body needs.

If you're in the habit of drinking a single glass of wine at bedtime, discuss with your doctor whether it's doing more good than harm under the current circumstances. If you find some nights you just can't relax enough to fall asleep, consult your doctor about prescribing something on a temporary basis.

EATING

APPETITE LOSS

> *"It feels like nothing will ever taste good again."*

> *"I wish people would stop presuring me to eat. I just don't feel hungry."*

> *"I know it's not very healthy, but the only thing that appeals to me right now is junk food."*

It's common for most people to feel a loss of appetite in the first month or so after the death. The body as well as the mind is in a state of shock. Appetite usually begins to return slowly with *time*. During this period, try to remember that your body needs fuel to function. Many people find several small snacks throughout the day are easier to manage than large meals. Try not to rush yourself or let others pressure you into eating. You may find yourself choosing "comfort foods", such as mashed potatoes, ice cream, etc. Consult your doctor about vitamin supplements and/or if your health is at risk by prolonged dietary changes.

OVEREATING

Sometimes food is the only thing that brings comfort. If you find yourself eating more than you normally do, chances are you're using food to soothe yourself during a painful time. Unless your doctor is concerned that your weight gain poses a health risk, don't try to diet right now. This is not the time to feel deprived again in any way. Remind yourself that the time will come when you will focus on your eating habits, but for now you may need the sense of comfort that food provides.

PAYING ATTENTION TO YOUR HEALTH

Grief is hard on your body. Intense emotions, eating and sleep disturbance, and having to cope with new and/or difficult situations can stress the body in ways that may surprise you. For those of you who had the additional strain of caring for your spouse before he or she died (sleepless nights, anxiety, dealing with the medical system, traveling to the hospital or clinic, etc.), it's important to accept that the wear and tear on your own health has been considerable.

It is easy to ignore your health, with so many changes in your life. *Don't.* This is a time you should pay attention to your body's welfare. When you're physically run-down, there's less resistance to colds and flu. Any preexisting medical problems may be affected by your current stress.

It is important to tell your physician you have recently suffered a major loss. Your doctor needs to be aware of any changes in your general health, especially if you have an ongoing medical condition.

IF YOU DO BECOME SICK

Suffering any illness following your spouse's death, whether it's a bad cold or something more serious, can be scary. As you experience yourself being physically vulnerable, the reality that your spouse is no longer around to take care of you can add to a painful sense of being alone in the world. Expect to feel increased anxiety at times like this.

* DON'T TRY TO BRAVE IT OUT. It's OK to let others know you're ill and need extra attention for a little while. People who care about you won't mind stopping by the drugstore, fixing a light meal, or just visiting on the phone.

* TRY TO RECALL ANYTHING YOUR SPOUSE SAID OR DID THAT WAS COMFORTING WHEN YOU WERE PREVIOUSLY ILL. Sometimes "hearing" your spouse's words of comfort can be reassuring.

* ARRANGE TO HAVE A FRIEND OR RELATIVE YOU CAN PHONE IF THE SITUATION GETS WORSE. Check to be sure they won't mind if you call in the middle of the night in case it becomes necessary. You probably won't need to call, but you'll sleep easier knowing someone is available.

* REALIZE THAT OTHERS MAY BECOME VERY ANXIOUS ABOUT YOUR ILLNESS. Children, even when they're adults, can become frightened when a surviving parent becomes sick. Assure them that you'll do everything possible to take care of yourself.

Chapter Four

Anxious About Being Anxious?

With all the upheaval in your life right now, it's normal to feel anxiety in one form or another. It may take the form of restlessness or feeling "jittery" at times. Or you might have a nagging sense of worry or even, under some circumstances, an experience of panic. The keys to managing anxiety are:

- TAKING THE TIME TO RECOGNIZE THAT YOU ARE ANXIOUS. Many people distract themselves by keeping busy, overeating, or trying not to think about what's bothering them.

- PINPOINTING THE CAUSE OF THE ANXIETY. Try to recall where and when you first became anxious. Being as specific as possible can help you uncover what's causing the fear or apprehension. You may discover that the worry isn't actually about a person or event but about how you'll cope with that particular person or event.

- LEARNING THAT ANXIETY CAN ACTUALLY HELP BY DRAWING ATTENTION TO SOMETHING YOU MAY NEED TO COPE WITH, TO SOOTHE, TO REASSURE, OR TO SOLVE. Once you're paying attention, you can make choices about how to deal with a particular anxiety-causing situation.

ANXIETY CHASERS

Many people never challenge the old perceptions they still have about themselves. They continue to believe deep down that they just aren't capable of handling what life sends their way. They're afraid they lack the ability to learn anything new. Ask yourself the following questions:

- Have I ever in my life been confronted by something new or extremely difficult that I've managed to deal with in a satisfactory way?

- Have I ever in my life been in this particular situation before? (Chances are you haven't, even though it may remind you of similar circumstances at some other time in your life.)

As you answer those questions, think about the following:

▶ LIFE IS A SERIES OF LEARNING EXPERIENCES, MANY OF WHICH I'VE ALREADY MASTERED. Some challenges are greater, and some struggles are harder than others; but, if I'm patient with and tolerant of myself, I know that somewhere within myself I'll find the qualities I already possess to deal with them.

▶ *REMEMBER: ALMOST NO ONE MASTERS SOMETHING NEW IMMEDIATELY.* Most people have to practice any new skill many times before they're comfortable with it. Think of all the activities you do every day but take for granted, such as driving a car. Remember the first time you tried to do these things? With practice you gained confidence.

- *IT'S OKAY TO ASK FOR HELP WHEN YOU NEED IT.*

- TAKE NOTES. Force yourself to stop, find a quiet place, and take out paper and pen. List everything that is worrying you at that moment. Then number each item from one to ten, with one indicating the most anxiety-provoking situation and ten the least. Choose one item, not necessarily the most difficult, and, on another page, write down at least two different ways you can approach that situation. It isn't necessary to follow through in tackling these situations, but the act of writing them down and reminding yourself you have choices in dealing with them will help reduce anxiety.

- *THOUGHT STOPPING/MAKING AN APPOINTMENT.* Often we brood over worrisome situations. The next time you find this happening, say to yourself (aloud if you're alone) "Stop!" or "Not now." Imagine yourself holding up a stop sign, and the troublesome thought suddenly halts in its tracks and disappears. Tell yourself that you'll tackle the problem by setting aside some time (from five to twenty minutes), when you can be alone in a quiet place to focus completely on the source of your anxiety. Write the time down as though you're making an appointment with yourself, and every time an anxious thought comes up, remind yourself to postpone dealing with it until it's scheduled.

- *NOTICE YOUR BODY.* Whenever you're anxious, you're also tense. Anxiety can affect your entire body. For example, as the muscles contract and tighten, breathing becomes irregular and shallow. Try this:

  - Find a quiet room and either sit comfortably or lie down.

  - Starting with your face, notice the tension in each muscle. Imagine yourself scanning the rest of your body for any signs of tension.

  - Close your eyes, and visualize yourself in a relaxing setting, like a forest or a lake.

  - Take a slow, deep breath, drawing air in through your nose. Hold it for a count of five, then slowly push the air out through your mouth. Repeat this breathing process five times.

- RELAXATION TAPES. Most libraries, music and book stores carry audio cassette tapes designed to help you relax. Some are recordings of natural settings, like the woods or the ocean, with a gentle musical accompaniment. Some add narration to guide you through a relaxation technique. These tapes are also helpful when you have trouble sleeping.

If worrying gets to the point where it's worrying you, consult your physician or a licensed counselor.

Chapter Five

Battling Guilt and Remorse

Guilt and remorse can be burdensome, as they force you to replay painful incidents over and over in your head. Every word and action is examined closely, and the punishment never seems to end.

These feelings can surface because of something you did or failed to do during your marriage or prior to your spouse's death. For many survivors, their helplessness to stop death from claiming their partner may be a major cause of guilt. To combat such feelings, try this unique approach:

REVISITING THE SCENE OF THE CRIME

1. Sit down alone in a quiet place with a pad of paper and pencil.

2. Imagine yourself in a different role: that of a detective observing a suspect (you at the time of the alleged crime). As the detective, it's important that you pay careful attention to any details that might have been previously overlooked.

3. As you picture the crime scene, answer the following questions (write them down so you can go back to them later):

* Where is the scene taking place? What time of day is it, and who else is present?

* Where was the suspect (as you were) just before the incident occurred? To whom, if anyone, were they talking, and what were they doing?

* How is the suspect feeling emotionally as the situation begins? Anxious or frightened or upset about something else?

* How is the suspect feeling physically? Suffering from a cold or exhausted from a lack of sleep?

* What other stresses or worries are going on in the suspect's life at the time?

4. Now look at your answers to the above questions and ask yourself: "Considering everything that was affecting me, what could I have done differently, realistically speaking, in that particular situation?"

Even if you did fail to take some action, can you make allowances for the fact that under these particular circumstances and at that moment, you struggled to do the best you could? If you failed to say something, can you remember any instance in the past when you either said or did something that was successfully communicated?

THE SENTENCE

Write a letter to your spouse about these feelings and/or discuss them with your spiritual advisor or counselor. If you find yourself continuing to think about those feelings or are preoccupied with intense guilt or remorse, seek the help of a professional counselor.

Chapter Six

Angry? Why Should I Be Angry?

When a spouse dies, it's common to feel some anger. You may not recognize it, but it's usually there. Anger, however, may feel especially uncomfortable when it occurs around a death. Many people feel guilty about acknowledging the anger.

> *"How can you be angry with someone for dying? After all, it's not like my spouse wanted to die."*

Although anger is a natural reaction to having lost your spouse, it may be easier to deal with it, if you give yourself permission to be angry that the loss happened. For example:

> *"It's so unfair that this had to happen to us!"*

Sometimes anger can cover up other, more difficult feelings, such as:

- **ABANDONMENT**

  "Why did she have to die and leave me? I always thought I'd be the first to go."

  or

  "Where are you when I need you?"

- **HELPLESSNESS**

  "I took such good care of her, but she died anyway."

  "I begged him to stop smoking/lose weight, but he just wouldn't listen!"

These reactions are understandable, if you keep in mind that death creates the ultimate experience of abandonment and helplessness.

> *"I wish everybody would stop fussing and just leave me alone. What's the use of going on, if my husband isn't here?"*

When anger is turned inward, it can take the form of depression or even suicidal feelings. If this is happening to you, see Chapter 7, **Suicidal Thoughts and Other Scary Stuff.**

"How could God let this happen to me?"

Some may undergo a religious crisis when their anger is directed at God. In questioning how God could allow their loved one to die, they experience this as a spiritual abandonment. For more on this, see Chapter 10, **Spiritual Comfort.**

Another common target for anger following a death is the medical establishment (doctors, nurses, hospital personnel). While there are certainly situations where anger toward a medical professional is justified, there are times when the real source of upset is the helplessness and frustration that come from not being able to stop the inevitable from occuring.

While it's important to be aware that you're feeling anger, it's equally important to look at what you are doing with it. Feeling an emotion and expressing it are two very different things. Everyone feels anger sometimes, but the way you choose to deal with that anger can make a world of difference. You'll probably feel angry and abandoned by your spouse when it comes time to deal with financial headaches, your children, family conflicts, etc. Misdirecting your anger in any way, such as yelling at your family for no reason, won't really make you feel better or less angry.

Here are some examples of choices you can make in handling anger:

DESTRUCTIVE WAYS	CONSTRUCTIVE WAYS
▼ Verbally or physically attacking others.	▼ Talking about your angry feelings to some one who will understand, such as close friends, grief counselors, bereavement groups or spiritual counselors.
▼ Turning anger inward. For example, scolding yourself, injuring your body by hitting something too hard, or having "accidents".	▼ Writing a letter to whomever you're angry with but not mailing it, then taking a brisk walk around the block.

- Doing self-destructive things like excessive drinking or drug use, driving recklessly, or neglecting your health.
- Punching a pillow or a cushioned piece of furniture.
- Sitting in a room at home with the windows closed (so the neighbors aren't alarmed) and yelling.

Chapter Seven

Suicidal Thoughts and Other Scary Stuff

SUICIDAL THOUGHTS

It's not uncommon for someone who has lost a spouse to feel so devastated that it seems at first as though life isn't worth continuing. The prospect of a future without your spouse, in which you see yourself unable to cope or find relief from a sense of pain and emptiness, can be terrifying.

For some, it's comforting to fantasize about being reunited in death with their lost partner. These thoughts are not unusual and, for most of you, will generally come briefly, at times when the pain of your loss is greatest. There's usually no intention of acting on this fantasy by actually ending your own life.

At these moments, remind yourself that over time, painful feelings will come and go. While you may not be able to change the fact that pain happens, you can become better skilled at handling the pain. There are *always* choices to make things more bearable. Suicide is an act that ends any possibility of these choices. Others have gone through this pain and have come out on the other side to a life that may also be fulfilling.

Some of you, however, may seriously think about taking your life. If you find yourself getting to that point:

- *Tell someone immediately!* Call the Operator to reach your local suicide hotline. Contact a mental health professional or talk to a trained religious counselor. You must get professional help whenever your feelings cause you to become a danger to yourself.

- *If suicide is a way to send a message to others, consider other options for expressing your anger or despair.* As hard as it may seem, telling others how we feel can often relieve our sense of distress. See Chapter 6, **Angry? Why Should I Be Angry?**

- *Consider the impact of suicide on your children.* Not only will you leave them without *any* parent to depend on, but studies show that they'll be at a much higher risk for suicide themselves. Is that the future you really want for your children? Is this the legacy you want to leave them?

- Remember: You are important! Get the help you need.

HALLUCINATIONS

> *"I was in the kitchen one day shortly after my wife died, when, suddenly, I thought I smelled her perfume. There wasn't a perfume bottle anywhere nearby, but the fragrance came to me very distinctly."*

Because bereavement is such an intense emotional experience, it's normal for your senses to occasionally play tricks on you. Many people report hearing, smelling, or even seeing their deceased spouse. For most of you, this experience can be very comforting.

Sometimes, however, hallucinations can continue to occur long after a loss or reflect images not related to your spouse. In most cases, overmedication or drug interaction can be the cause. It's important to check with your physician or mental health professional if hallucinations continue.

SENSE OF YOUR SPOUSE BEING PRESENT

> *"Last night I suddenly woke up and was sure I could feel my husband lying there next to me, just like always. It was so reassuring that I was afraid to turn and look, in case it was all in my imagination."*

Many have reported finding solace in having "conversations" with their deceased spouse. When you've lived with another person for a long time, their presence becomes a part of your physical landscape. Each room holds associations and memories of that person. It's not uncommon, then, for many people to experience a sense of their spouse's presence from time to time. When this occurs, it can give you a comforting sense of connection to your spouse in the early period after their death. It usually goes away with time.

BEREAVEMENT VERSUS MAJOR DEPRESSION

Often people tend to confuse normal bereavement, which is important to go through, with an episode of major depression. That's understandable, because many of the symptoms (for example sadness, appetite and energy loss, and an inability to enjoy what used to give you pleasure), appear similar. It's important to understand the differences, however, because that awareness can influence the way you deal with the symptoms.

NORMAL BEREAVEMENT	MAJOR DEPRESSION
▼ Reaction to an actual recent death.	▼ Reaction to various causes i.e., a life transition (such as children leaving home), a situation (such as losing a job, moving), or childhood trauma.
▼ a normal, natural emotional process that needs to be given sufficient time to be completed.	▼ An emotional disorder that requires the identification of underlying causes and treatment of symptoms by a professional. The goal of treatment is to stop the emotional distress as quickly as possible.

It's possible to experience major depression while you're also grieving a recent loss. As a result of your spouse's death, you may find yourself struggling with additional emotional stresses of financial or family problems. A mental health professional can be especially useful in helping you sort through this.

MULTIPLE LOSSES AND PREVIOUS LOSSES

If you've experienced more than one death within the last few years, it's important to give yourself *more* time to go through the grieving process. Sometimes another death occurs before you've had sufficient time to grieve the earlier loss adequately. You may feel overwhelmed. Give yourself permission to take your time.

With every loss a person experiences, previous losses may come up in some way. If you find yourself talking about someone else you lost long ago, it could be a sign that an old loss is being felt again.

MEDICATION

It is important to discover whether you're experiencing normal bereavement or major depression, because medication for depression can possibly hinder the natural process of grief. It does this by stalling the ebb and flow of emotions necessary to the successful completion of bereavement. Many well-meaning physicians have prescribed antidepressant medication for normal bereavement, only to have their patients return time after time with the same distress, never having completed the mourning process.

If, however, you find you need something to get through the sleeplessness and appetite loss of bereavement, consult your physician about taking medication on a *temporary* basis.

If you're concerned about other symptoms, such as persistent hallucinations, you may be referred to a psychiatrist. Seeing a psychiatrist does not mean you're crazy or mentally ill. As physicians who specialize in evaluating and treating different types of depression, psychiatrists are best able to prescribe the right medication for your emotional distress, in addition to providing psychotherapy.

Chapter Eight

Now Where Did I Leave Those Car Keys?

"Since my husband died, I've gotten so forgetful and absentminded. I'm frightened that maybe I've got Alzheimer's or something."

After a major loss, you're dealing with intense thoughts and emotions. You may still be in a state of shock and hindered by a lack of sleep. Because of being overloaded, the mind often cannot process information in its usual way. It's normal, therefore, to experience some temporary trouble remembering things. The important point is that you haven't lost your memory; it just takes longer to retrieve information.

> *"I arrived at my destination but momentarily found myself unsure about where I was or how I'd gotten there. It was scary."*

Feeling "spaced out" or disoriented about where you are or what day of the week it is is also normal and temporary. The length of time you'll experience problems with memory and orientation may depend on whether your loss was anticipated or happened suddenly. It generally takes more time to come to terms with an unexpected loss.

Meanwhile, try not to panic. Here's what we suggest:

- GIVE YOURSELF PERMISSION. Remember that for now, *not normal is normal*. The memory and sense of orientation that you've always taken for granted are not the same during this period. Even the most conscientious people become forgetful and at times confused when they've suffered a major loss.

- IF YOU FIND YOU'VE LOST TRACK OF SOMETHING, STOP. TAKE THREE DEEP BREATHS AND MENTALLY RETRACE YOUR STEPS. If necessary, actually return to each location you previously visited.

- WRITE THINGS DOWN. Whenever you make an appointment, it's wise to immediately make a note of the time and place that's been scheduled. Many people take notes during discussions when important information is being covered.

- SET UP SEVERAL "INFORMATION CENTERS" IN DIFFERENT ROOMS. These could be desks, refrigerators, or other objects you pass by frequently. High *visibility* is the key.

- USE DIFFERENT COLORED STICKY NOTES TO ALERT YOURSELF TO WHAT NEEDS IMMEDIATE ATTENTION AND WHAT CAN WAIT. You might, for example, use hot pink or yellow note paper to remind yourself of an urgent errand or to pay certain bills. Stick these notes on an information center and remove them once you've taken care of each situation.

- PURCHASE SEVERAL SPARE KEYS. Keep extra keys at your various information centers or wear them on your person.

CHAPTER NINE

My Loss Didn't Happen In The Usual Way

Most of the deaths we've been referring to in this book are assumed to be caused by health-related conditions, such as cancer or heart conditions. Some of you, however, may have special circumstances involved in your spouse's loss and need to be aware of how that could affect your bereavement experience.

SUICIDE

> *"She seemed okay. Why didn't she tell me she was feeling so depressed?"*
>
> *"He often said life wasn't worthwhile, but I didn't think he'd ever kill himself."*

The aftermath of suicide can be especially difficult to cope with, because it can leave you, as a survivor, feeling:

* Confused, guilty, and self-blaming about why this act was committed and that you may have been responsible.

* Believing that you weren't valuable and/or powerful enough to prevent someone choosing to die.

* Shamed by the attitude and questions of family, friends and the police.

* Concerned about your clergyman's reaction, as some religions regard suicide as a sin.

* Worried about what to tell your child about the circumstances.

Expect your grieving process to take somewhat longer, because of the added burden of all of the above. Here, however, are some ways to make it easier on yourself:

YOUR SPOUSE EXERCISED A CHOICE AND ULTIMATELY WAS THE ONLY ONE TO HAVE THE POWER TO ACT ON THAT CHOICE. If there was anger at you or anyone else, there were other more effective ways he/she could have chosen to communicate feelings.

YOU ARE NOT TO BLAME FOR SOMETHING AS COMPLEX AS ANOTHER PERSON'S ACT OF SUICIDE. A multitude of factors, such as personality, self-esteem, family history, and the ability to deal with life's stresses all contributed to your spouse's behavior.

YOU MAY BE TURNING THE ANGER YOU FEEL ABOUT YOUR SPOUSE'S ABANDONMENT INWARD ONTO YOURSELF. This can take the form of guilt and self-blame at being helpless to stop a suicide. It is not disloyal to be angry at people we love when their actions cause us pain.

A SUICIDE NOTE REFLECTS ONLY WHAT YOUR SPOUSE HAPPENED TO BE FEELING AT THE TIME IT WAS WRITTEN. Try not to view it as a generalization about your entire past relationship.

CHILDREN TEND TO BLAME THEMSELVES WHEN A PARENT DIES, EVEN THOUGH THEY MAY NOT EXPRESS IT OPENLY OR BE AWARE OF IT THEMSELVES. Recognizing this can be difficult; because, unlike most adults, children show they're upset by their behavior, rather than by talking. A child may be especially prone to self-blame, in the case of suicide. Children need to be given simple, truthful explanations of what has happened. It's also best to tell them how it happened, or they will fantasize about all sorts of frightening possibilites.

BECAUSE IT'S COMMON FOR FAMILY MEMBERS TO BLAME THE SURVIVING SPOUSE FOR EITHER CAUSING OR NOT PREVENTING THE SUICIDE, IT'S HELPFUL TO TALK ABOUT YOUR FEELINGS WITH SUPPORTIVE PEOPLE OUTSIDE OF YOUR FAMILY. Join a support group, if there is one available.

DESPITE THE FEELINGS OF SHAME IT MAY BRING UP, IT IS BEST TO BE TRUTHFUL WITH YOURSELF AND OTHERS ABOUT THE REASONS YOUR SPOUSE DIED. Creating a face-saving "cover-up" story will only complicate and further delay working through your bereavement process.

AS CLERGY, IN GENERAL, HAVE BECOME MORE AWARE OF AND INFLUENCED BY THE FIELD OF PSYCHOLOGY AND SUICIDOLOGY, THEY'VE DEVELOPED MORE SENSITIVITY TO THE ISSUE OF SUICIDE. If you are otherwise comfortable talking with your clergy, you can turn to them despite an "official" doctrine about suicide.

WRITE YOUR FEELINGS IN A JOURNAL OR AS A LETTER TO YOUR SPOUSE.

WHEN YOU THINK YOUR SPOUSE CONTRIBUTED IN SOME WAY TOWARD THEIR OWN DEATH

> *"No matter how many times the doctor warned him, and I begged, threatened and tried to help, he still ignored us."*

If your spouse's death occurred as an apparent result of not following medical advice and/or complying with treatment or substance abuse, it can seem that he/she chose to die. While the term "suicide" is generally applied to a sudden act that results in death, these situations can seem like a form of slow suicide.

You may find yourself relating to some of the reactions described in the above section, with one difference: in this instance, you probably feel more anger than guilt. After what may have been years of frustration as you tried your best to control your spouse's self-destructive behavior, he/she died anyway. As a consequence, you see yourself as not having been valuable or powerful enough in the relationship to stop your spouse's downward spiral.

As we said earlier, self-destruction is a complicated matter, with a multitude of influences.

DEATH BY ACCIDENT

> *"It all seems so unreal. He kissed me goodbye, drove off to work just like he always does, and now he's dead."*

The suddenness of a death caused by an accident can present some special concerns for the surviving spouse:

WITH ANY SUDDEN DEATH, THERE IS ALMOST ALWAYS UNFINISHED BUSINESS: UNRESOLVED CONFLICTS, WORDS EITHER SPOKEN IN ANGER OR NOT AT ALL, PLANS LEFT UNCLEAR OR INCOMPLETE. You are cheated of the opportunity to put things in order before the finality of death.

WHEN DEATH COMES UNEXPECTEDLY, IT SEEMS UNREAL, LIKE A BAD DREAM THAT WILL BE OVER ONCE YOU WAKE UP. Expect this sense of unreality to persist for awhile.

YOU HAVE TO STRUGGLE WITH A SENSE OF HELPLESSNESS, AS EVENTS FOLLOWING THE DEATH MOVE YOU ALONG WITH THEM. With an accidental death, there is often a need to place blame somewhere.

YOUR ABILITY TO GRIEVE YOUR LOSS MAY BE DELAYED BY LEGAL AND/OR MEDICAL BUSINESS. Months and sometimes years of dealing with the police, attorneys, physicians and the courts can interfere with your bereavement.

YOU MAY FEEL RAGE OVER THE UNFAIRNESS OF WHAT HAS HAPPENED. This type of death can threaten your deepest sense of safety about the world as well as your basic assumptions about fairness and justice. If there is a trial, any possible disillusionment about the legal system can also fuel this sense of rage.

IN ADDITION TO ALL OF THE ABOVE, YOU MAY BE FORCED TO COPE WITH THE INTRUSION OF THE MEDIA. Since this usually occurs shortly after a death, when you and your family are still in a state of shock, being asked to share your intimate reactions in such a public way can be experienced as a violation.

DEATH BY HOMICIDE

"Since the moment the police came to the door and told me my husband was murdered, I've felt trapped in a nightmare and can't wake up."

When a death is due to murder, there are some particularly painful issues to be dealt with. In addition to many of the concerns associated with any sudden death, you'll probably find yourself struggling with some of the following:

BECAUSE OF THE INTENSE PUBLIC REACTION THAT OFTEN ACCOMPANIES NEWS OF A MURDER, THE INTRUSION OF THE MEDIA CAN FEEL ESPECIALLY OVERWHELMING. Awkward and/or probing questions about the situation by curious friends and neighbors can also feel invasive and alienating. Remember, you don't have to respond to any questions, if you don't wish to.

A SENSE OF ISOLATION AND BEING DIFFERENT FROM MOST OTHER PEOPLE.

A HOMICIDE ISN'T FINISHED UNTIL SOMETHING HAPPENS TO BRING CLOSURE. Forced by circumstances to depend upon the legal system to catch and try the murderer, you are probably feeling rage about being helpless, cheated and stuck in an emotional limbo. In a situation where the murderer can't be found, your sense of helplessness may feel unbearable at times.

YOU MAY BE ASKED TO BE A PART OF THE LEGAL PROCEEDINGS. In addition to slowing your ability to grieve, going through a trial can reactivate the trauma of the death. Try to surround yourself with as much emotional support as possible. The Victims of Crime Program in your area can provide volunteers to be with you during a trial.

If you haven't already been involved with this program, (it's customary for homicide detectives and/or the District Attorney's office to offer this resource), ask the information operator or local police for the telephone number.

WHEN THE BODY CAN'T BE RETRIEVED

> *"The crash was almost a year ago, and they still haven't found any trace of my husband's body. You can't imagine how agonizing it is to have your entire life in limbo like this."*

Enduring years of uncertainty while you wait for your spouse's remains to be recovered can be an especially painful ordeal. In some cases, you are facing seven years in legal, financial, and emotional limbo before a death certificate can be issued and you're "officially" widowed.

In addition to not being able to collect death benefits (you need a death certificate to do so), the time and emotional energy spent in the search itself, legal hassles, and paperwork delay your opportunity to grieve for your spouse fully. Many people in these circumstances find that at a certain point, it helps to hold a memorial service for the deceased. Acknowledging loss openly in this way, with the comforting support of family and friends, can be an important step towards working through your grief.

Part Two

Getting Through The Days

CHAPTER TEN

Spiritual Comfort

For some, bereavement is a time when religion provides great comfort and support. For others, it can be a painful time in which you question your most cherished beliefs. The impact of losing a spouse can cause some people to experience a crisis of faith. In the face of death, each of us struggles in his or her own way to find answers to profoundly difficult questions. You may question the fairness of the loss:

> *"We played by the rules. My spouse was such a good, loving person. Why did this have to happen to us?"*

You may feel that death cheated you of many things: your spouse as your life partner, the dreams and plans you had for the future, the sharing of family experiences.

It's not uncommon to feel anger toward God for allowing the loss to happen. While some people feel guilt about expressing it, others find relief by allowing themselves to vent this anger directly at God. Some may even shake their fists at the heavens. Still others may turn away from their religion.

COMING TO TERMS WITH THE QUESTIONS

Each faith has its own way of understanding the experience of death. Some people turn to their spiritual advisor and find answers that are comforting. Others may be given answers that fail to satisfy them when they're feeling such terrible pain. This can feel like an even more profound loss.

Before you decide to give up on your faith:

- GIVE YOURSELF TIME. Some have to struggle for awhile before they discover answers that feel right.

- GET A DIFFERENT PERSPECTIVE. Some clergy are simply more skillful at handling these issues than others. Rather than giving up on your faith, you might want to consider consulting another clerical member of your denomination. Sometimes another perspective (and personality) can make all the difference.

Other good sources of comfort are books that deal with the "whys". See Chapter 24, **Resources For Help Along The Way**, for suggestions.

CHAPTER ELEVEN

You're Young and Lost Your Partner

No matter how many years you've been married, it probably feels as if you didn't have enough time together. Being younger when this happens can create additional anxiety and isolation.

Here are some common issues confronting younger surviving spouses:

LOSING A SPOUSE IS UNEXPECTED. You didn't expect to lose a spouse while you're still young. Decisions about the future were probably made with the assumption there would be many more productive working years ahead. This often means you're left financially unprepared.

FEW (IF ANY) OF YOUR PEERS HAVE LOST THEIR HUSBANDS OR WIVES. Not having anyone your own age to share your bereavement experience can make you feel isolated and "different".

HAVING TO RAISE CHILDREN BY YOURSELF. Juggling your children's emotional and physical needs as well as your own can overwhelm you as the sole parent. Men, especially, may be confronted by the sudden need for child care or a live-in housekeeper.

PRESSURE AND LACK OF UNDERSTANDING FROM OTHERS. Because your loss has occurred early in life, there could be an expectation from others (and maybe yourself) that you can "bounce back" more quickly than if the loss had happened at a later age. Within a short time after the death, well-meaning friends and family may urge you to "get on with your life" and push you into dating before you are ready.

LOSS BY DIVORCE IS NOT THE SAME AS LOSS BY DEATH. The loss of a spouse by death is a different experience. No matter how ugly a divorce, at least the spouse is still alive. Death, however, is final.

TAKING CARE OF YOURSELF

Here are some ways to cope with the above issues:

- Accept that you have to rethink and create a new plan for your financial future. If you need help in understanding monetary details or making decisions, ask someone you trust for advice. Allow yourself as much time as possible before taking any major steps. Think about the possibility of some temporary help with expenses from family or friends.

IMPORTANT NOTE: If you must look for a job right away, keep in mind that for now, you'll probably do best working at something that involves a minimum of mental stress. If you're already working, see Chapter 15, **Back To Work.**

- Look for a bereavement group that specifically deals with younger spouses. Don't rule out the possibility of a group with older members. Although there will be some differences, the basic experience is the same, and sharing those common feelings can be comforting.

- For support in coping with the demands of single parenthood, consider joining a parents' group such as Parents Without Partners or those offered by many schools, community centers, and churches or synagogues.

For support in understanding and dealing with your child's reaction to the death of your spouse, see Chapter 12, **Your Child's Reactions.**

IMPORTANT NOTE: It's extremely important, especially if you have children, to give yourself some time alone every day. Once you've had a chance to "let down" and grieve or just unwind from the day's pressures, you'll be better able to give your children the attention they need.

- Remind youself and anyone who's pressuring you about dating that you are the best authority on what's right for you. It is important to give yourself as much time as you need before taking this step. Once you've decided to begin dating, remember: don't rush into anything. While the loss of companionship and a sex life can seem unbearable at times, the consequences of trying to short-circuit the pain of grieving will eventually catch up with you. Before going ahead with dating, we suggest you read Chapter 22, **Am I Really Ready For This?**

▶ A FINAL NOTE: You are especially vulnerable right now. There are people out there who prey on the recently widowed. Be cautious!

- Those who have gone through a divorce may try to console you by relating their own experiences and saying they understand yours. Sometimes they will; sometimes they won't. In the latter instance, you might want to respond with something like this:

  "I realize you are trying to understand what I'm going through right now, and I really appreciate it. While both are painful losses, having a marriage end because of death is very different from having it end in divorce. Death is final."

CHAPTER TWELVE

Your Child's Reactions

When a parent dies, a child's world is impacted in a number of ways:

* Children expect their parents to always be there.

* The surviving and grieving parent is often emotionally unavailable to them. Your child may be afraid of showing distress out of fear of further upsetting you.

* A child may also feel that other adults and children suddenly act differently toward them.

* Other people are often uncertain about how to respond to a child.

MAKING SENSE OF DEATH

"Mommy, where did Daddy go? Is he coming back?"

Your child's age at the time of the death determines how they understand what has occurred. For most children under the age of seven, it is difficult to make sense of death. There is often some confusion about what has actually happened, and you may see a young child struggle to understand the reality of death. This doesn't mean, however, that young children don't feel the loss or think about and miss the deceased parent.

Whatever your beliefs are about death, try to explain them in ways that are clear and won't leave your child puzzled or frightened. Always let your child know that any of his or her feelings about the death are normal and OK. You might, for example, say something like this to a younger child:

> *"Daddy's in heaven with God now, and he isn't ever going to come back. We're all going to miss Daddy very, very much and feel upset and cry for awhile. We'll never forget Daddy or how much he loved us. I also want you to know that Mommy isn't going to leave you. I'll be right here to love you and take care of you."*

The first sentence can be modified to reflect a nonreligious approach:

> *"Daddy/Mommy has died, and he or she isn't ever going to come back."*

CHILDREN AND ADOLESCENTS

> "As far as I can tell, my daughter's handling things pretty well. Apart from some tears and a few questions when I told her her daddy died, she seems to be her usual happy-go-lucky self. I have noticed she's wetting the bed again, though, but don't all kids do that sort of thing sometimes? Anyway, with every-

thing else going on, I'm just too overwhelmed to pay much attention to that sort of thing right now."

"My son has started spending most of his time holed up alone in his room with the music blaring. I've tried a few times to talk to him about the loss, but he just ignores me. I'm ready to give up."

While you're caught up in the pain and upheaval of your own grieving, it can be hard for you to understand or have patience for the ways in which a child or adolescent is grieving. It's important to realize that like you, children and adolescents grieve in their own unique ways. There are, however, some important differences in how children grieve.

For you, bereavement is at first very intense with the loss being felt almost constantly, but then the pain gradually eases. For your child, grieving tends to come and go. This can create the impression that your child is either "over" the loss quickly or perhaps feels it less strongly than you do. That isn't true. Remember that while adults can *tell* others what they're feeling, children and adolescents usually *show* their reactions in their *behavior*.

Some common reactions to watch for in children include:

- *WITHDRAWING AND/OR APPEARING TO HAVE FEELINGS OF SHAME OR INADEQUACY.*

- *SCHOOL PROBLEMS.*

- *INCREASED AGGRESSIVENESS: HITTING, FIGHTING, OR BREAKING THINGS.*

- *A RETURN TO EARLIER BEHAVIOR LIKE BED-WETTING, THUMB-SUCKING, BABY-TALK, OR CRAWLING.* This reflects the child's wish to go back to a safer time in their lives.

- *CLINGING, ANXIOUS BEHAVIOR.*

- *SEARCHING FOR THE LOST PARENT.*

- *BLAMING THE SURVIVING PARENT FOR THE LOSS.* Your child may hold you responsible for not preventing the death.

- FRIGHTENING DREAMS AND/OR WANTING TO GET INTO BED WITH YOU AT NIGHT.

Changes to be aware of in adolescents include:

- *MORE THAN USUAL WITHDRAWAL FROM FAMILY AND POSSIBLY FRIENDS.*

- *UNUSUAL WEIGHT GAIN OR LOSS.*

- *BLAMING THE SURVIVING PARENT FOR THE LOSS.* Your adolescent may hold you responsible for not preventing the death.

- PROBLEMS AT SCHOOL, SUCH AS POOR PERFORMANCE OR TRUANCY.

- AGGRESSIVE BEHAVIOR, SUCH AS HITTING WALLS, PICKING FIGHTS, DESTROYING PROPERTY OR GETTING INTO TROUBLE WITH THE LAW. Adolescents often focus their anger on people closest to them.

- *SUBSTANCE ABUSE*

- *SUICIDAL IDEAS OR EVEN ATTEMPTS*. This is usually an attempt to express anger at the death and play out a fantasy of being reunited with the dead parent.

► IMPORTANT NOTE: If your daughter or son of any age is talking about suicide or seems likely to make an attempt, get professional help *right away*. Call the Operator, (who will connect you to the suicide hot line), contact your local child guidance clinic or ask your pediatrician for a referral to a qualified mental health professional.

You may become angry or want to punish your child or adolescent for any of the above behavior. Or, you may just want to ignore it in the hope it will go away. We suggest, instead, you try to understand that this behavior is your child's attempt to deal with some very powerful, often frightening emotions that he/she is unable to talk about. Your child needs you, as well as other supportive adults, to help find words to express the pain. In fact, it's crucial to enlist the help of other caring adults to help your child work through the bereavement process. Trusted family and neighbors can be invaluable at a time when you're so overwhelmed.

Here, then, are many of the normal feelings your child or adolescent may be experiencing but unable to put into words:

- *FEAR OF ABANDONMENT*

  "Who's going to take care of me now that Mommy's not here?"

- *GUILT AND/OR REMORSE*

  "It's my fault Dad's dead. We had a really horrible fight the night before, and he got so stressed out it killed him."

- *ANGER*

  "Why me? Why did I have to be the one to lose my Mom? All of my friends still have their moms!"

- *ANXIETY*

  "I'm scared in my room, Mommy. Can't I sleep in your bed?"

- *DEPRESSION*

  "I don't feel like playing with anybody. I'm too sad."

- *LONGING FOR THE DECEASED PARENT*

  "Who just called on the telephone? I'll bet it was Mommy calling to tell us she's coming back?"

- A SENSE OF FEELING "CRAZY"

  "Sometimes I feel like I'm gonna just freak out and start screaming at the whole world."

- *A SENSE OF SHAME*

  "I'm different and not as good as the other kids."

- *FEELINGS OF HELPLESSNESS*

"How will I ever learn to drive, now that Dad's gone?"

► IMPORTANT NOTE: The two main emotional issues for children and adolescents are *abandonment* happening again and *guilt.* ("They died because I was bad.") These thoughts lie behind many of the above reactions.

A WORD ABOUT SHOWING YOUR OWN GRIEF: You may worry about whether it's OK to let your child see you grieve; and, if so, how should you handle the situation? Since some display of your pain in front of your child is unavoidable, we suggest that whenever it occurs, you say something like this:

> "I know it's hard to see Mommy cry, but she's feeling very sad, and crying helps the sadness get better. Even though she's sad, Mommy still loves you. It's OK if you feel sad and need to cry, too."

This also gives the child the message that it's good to express emotions, and that crying is a healthy way to release feelings.

TIPS FOR HELPING YOUR CHILD COPE

PRESCHOOL AGE

REMEMBER THAT IT'S NORMAL FOR THERE TO BE A RETURN TO EARLIER BEHAVIOR LIKE BABY-TALK, BED-WETTING, ETC.

REASSURE AND TRY TO HELP YOUR CHILD FIND WORDS FOR HOW SCARED, WORRIED, ETC. THEY MAY BE. Use puppets, dolls, drawings, and books to give your child an opportunity to express grief. See Chapter 24, **Resources For Help Along The Way** for suggested books for children.

YOUNG CHILDREN ARE EXTREMELY CONCRETE IN HOW THEY UNDERSTAND THINGS. When discussing the death, try to be very clear and simple in your explanations to avoid creating confusion and increased anxiety for your child.

THE PERMANENCE OF DEATH IS ESPECIALLY HARD FOR YOUNGER CHILDREN TO GRASP. If you find your child asking, "When is Mommy/Daddy coming back?", here's an example of how you might reply: "You wish Mommy/Daddy were coming back, but they aren't. It makes me really sad too. It's OK for you to be sad and cry. We both miss her/him very much."

CHECK WITH YOUR LOCAL CHILD GUIDANCE SERVICES ABOUT A BEREAVEMENT GROUP OR PROGRAM GEARED FOR YOUNGER CHILDREN. See Chapter 24, **Resources For Help Along The Way.** *It is even more important to obtain help for a child who says nothing about the death.*

OLDER CHILDREN

TRY TO MAINTAIN AS MUCH OF A NORMAL ROUTINE AS POSSIBLE. ALL CHILDREN AS WELL AS ADOLESCENTS ARE REASSURED BY KNOWING THAT IN THE MIDST OF ALL THE OTHER

CHANGES, SOME THINGS REMAIN SAFE AND STEADY. Try to maintain the usual rules.

EXPECT SOME RETURN TO EARLIER BEHAVIOR. It can also be helpful to use drawings, toys and books to help older children express their feelings.

YOUR CHILD WILL PROBABLY BE ANXIOUS TO RETURN TO SCHOOL. This is your child's daily world and a much needed source of support for them during this time. In addition to the stability it provides, it's where friends and teachers can offer an ear for feelings your child may hesitate to share with you.

BEFORE YOUR CHILD RETURNS TO SCHOOL, CONTACT HIS/HER TEACHER AND THE SCHOOL COUNSELOR AND DISCUSS HOW THEY CAN TELL YOUR CHILD'S CLASSMATES ABOUT THE DEATH BEFORE YOUR CHILD RETURNS. It's important the teacher be aware that your child's loss may stir up fears in other children about losing a parent. The teacher might also explore with your child and his/her classmates how to respond supportively when your child becomes sad or tearful.

ARRANGE AHEAD OF TIME FOR YOU OR ANOTHER ADULT TO COME TO PICK UP YOUR CHILD FROM SCHOOL, IF BEING THERE BECOMES TOO OVERWHELMING.

CONTACT THE PARENTS OF YOUR CHILD'S PLAYMATES ABOUT THE DEATH AND SUGGEST THEY TALK TO THEIR CHILDREN ABOUT WHAT HAS HAPPENED AND HOW THEY CAN PROVIDE REASSURANCE.

ALTHOUGH IT MAY BE DIFFICULT FOR YOU, AT SOME POINT CREATE A "MEMORY BOOK" WITH YOUR CHILD. Gather photos of your wedding, baby pictures that include your spouse, and anything else that holds special memories of your spouse for your child. Put these together into a book that your child can turn to as a way of remembering and grieving for the lost parent.

ADOLESCENTS

BECAUSE ADOLESCENCE IS A TIME OF LIFE FULL OF CONFLICT WHEN A CHILD BEGINS TO PULL AWAY FROM THE PARENT, YOUR TEENAGER MAY BE HAVING VERY MIXED FEELINGS ABOUT HIS OR HER LOST PARENT. There's frequently anger toward the dead parent as well as guilt about feeling that anger. Try to let your teenagers know you don't blame them for the way they may have acted toward your spouse, and that friction between parents and teens is normal. Tell them it's OK to feel angry about being abandoned, especially at a point where there hasn't been enough time to resolve areas of dispute. Reassure them that all their feelings are OK and understandable in light of what's happened.

IF YOUR TEENAGER WANTS TO JOIN HIS OR HER FRIENDS AND GO TO A MOVIE THE DAY AFTER THE FUNERAL, LET THEM. Remember, their friends are like another family to them and offer additional emotional support at a time when you are involved in your own grieving.

ASK YOUR TEENAGER IF HE/SHE WOULD LIKE YOU TO INFORM THE SCHOOL OR ANY TEACHERS ABOUT THE DEATH. This is to ensure that the teacher will be understanding of the change in behavior and school work. Let your teenager tell classmates and friends in his or her own way, if they prefer to do so.

FIND A BEREAVEMENT GROUP FOR ADOLESCENTS WHO HAVE LOST A PARENT. See Chapter 24, **Resources For Help Along The Way.**

BRINGING A CARETAKER/HOUSEKEEPER INTO YOUR HOME

Introducing an unfamiliar person into the household following your spouse's death can present special concerns in terms of your child's sense of emotional security. It's important that the caretaker/housekeeper be made aware of the following:

THE IMPORTANCE OF BEING SENSITIVE TO YOUR CHILD'S GRIEVING. Explain that your child's behavior may sometimes reflect the inability to talk about the loss.

HOW TO HANDLE ISSUES OF LOSS. Clarify that you wish your own beliefs about death and loss, rather than the caretaker's, to be the response to your child's questions or concerns. If the caretaker is of a different religion and hence, views death differently, it might be wise to discuss the family's religious orientation with him/her.

YOUR CHILD'S NEEDS AND CONCERNS REGARDING HOUSEHOLD ROUTINES. Allowing your child to participate in a discussion on this subject will help him or her feel understood by the new person caring for them.

A FINAL WORD ON THE SUBJECT OF FUNERALS

Although most of you will probably be reading this book some time after the funeral has occurred, some of you may be facing that experience and wondering whether or not to have your child attend.

Whether a child attends his or her parent's funeral depends upon the child, his/her age and level of understanding. Customs vary in terms of how funerals are conducted and how mourners show their grief at the event. Unless a younger child has already attended a family funeral, he or she may become frighted by all the strange procedures and emotional loss of control unfolding before them.

It's important to tell a child before the service whether the casket will be open for viewing or closed. If it will be open, explain that family and friends may touch or perhaps kiss the deceased. If closed, explain that there will be no longer opportunity to see the parent. This allows time for the child to express any feelings or concerns that should be respected in the situation.

With any child, it's a good idea to describe what will be happening. If your child does attend, ask a friend or family member (who won't mind missing some of the service) to "keep an eye on" your child in case he/she becomes uncomfortable and needs to "take a walk and talk about things". This way, you can focus on getting through the day without having to worry that your child's needs aren't being addressed.

With adequate emotional support, the opportunity to observe a funeral and see others confronting loss can make it easier for a child to accept the death of a parent. Once the event is over, sit down with your child and in a clear, sensitive way, describe what went on. They might find drawing pictures helpful.

CHAPTER THIRTEEN

People Do Need People

HELP FROM OTHERS

As you struggle with the emotional stress and added responsibilities that come with losing your spouse, there are times you need help from family and/or friends. While they are usually more than willing to offer support, you may feel uncomfortable accepting assistance. It can be unsettling to find yourself needing help with those things you have usually managed on your own.

You may fear the possibility of becoming a burden, especially on family. If depending on others is difficult for you, consider the following points:

> *Bereavement is a time when people do need people.*
>
> YOUR LIMITATIONS IN COPING ARE TEMPORARY. With time, you'll get better at handling new responsibilities.
>
> THIS IS A TIME WHEN EVEN THE SIMPLEST TASK CAN FEEL OVERWHELMING, SO GIVE YOURSELF PERMISSION TO ALLOW OTHERS TO HELP.

If you have difficulty turning to others for help, ask yourself, "If the situation were reversed, wouldn't I be there for them?"

Delegate the tasks you need help with to several people. Many people find this approach helps lessen worry about overburdening one particular person.

Communicate as directly as possible when you need someone's help. In phoning a friend, for example, you might say, "With everything that's going on right now, I'm feeling a little overwhelmed. I was wondering if you'd mind helping me with ..."

Keep in mind that most people are eager to help. Lending you a hand will make them feel less helpless and good about "doing something" for you, even if it's only picking up a few groceries for you.

WHEN THERE'S MORE HELP THAN YOU WANT

In the period right after your spouse's death, having friends and family step in and take over responsibilities may be a relief. As you begin to regain your ability to cope, however, too much "help" may leave you uncomfortable. So how do you tell someone you need less of their help but still need to know you can count on them when the occasion arises?

Here is an example of one approach:

> *"I want you to know how much your help has meant, but I'm beginning to feel stronger, and it's important*

for me to begin to stand on my own two feet when possible. There may still be times when I need your help. Would it be okay if I called you?"

Here is another:

"Thanks for all the help you've given me. I'm feeling more like my old self. If anything else comes up that I can't handle, may I let you know?"

TO JOIN OR NOT TO JOIN A BEREAVEMENT GROUP

Many churches, synagogues, hospitals and others provide free or low-fee nondenominational support groups for the bereaved. If such a group is being offered in your area, consider at least giving it a try. A group can be a wonderful place to meet others who are in the same boat and experiencing feelings similar to yours. Through listening to "other people's problems," you'll feel less alone. You may be interested in joining but are hesitant to actually show up because of some of these common concerns:

"I don't want to listen to other people's problems ... I have enough of my own."

or

"I'm not sure if I can talk about myself in front of other people. I'm a private kind of person."

After hearing other group members share their experiences, you'll probably become more comfortable talking about your own. It's important, too, to check ahead of time about confidentiality.

If it's a group rule, then nothing you share should be discussed by any other member outside of the group.

> *"Since we're talking about such a depressing subject, won't everybody be crying all the time?"*

As hard as it may be to believe, there are usually more moments of laughter than tears in a bereavement group.

> *"What if I break down and start crying in front of everybody?"*

Many people will be embarrassed if they cry or worry about how it will look if they don't. Once you've given yourself time to get comfortable in a group, you'll be reassured by the support of others in the same boat.

Here's something else to consider: a group can provide a good place to say those things which would be a burden if said to friends or family members.

In our experience, a well-run group allows everyone to feel at ease. The comfort and reassurance you'll gain will quickly outweigh any initial uneasiness you feel.

GROUPS VERSUS INDIVIDUAL GRIEF COUNSELING

You may receive a lot of well-meaning advice from family and friends who may have either been in groups or one-on-one counseling with a religious counselor or psychotherapist. If you are looking for support in coping with your bereavement, it's helpful to understand some basic differences in the form that support takes:

* A SUPPORT GROUP involves a gathering of others (size of the group may vary) who have lost their spouse or, in some cases, other loved ones. Under the guidance of a trained group leader, members of the group share their experiences of loss and offer emotional support when others talk about their experiences. Most people say a group helps them feel less alone and reassures them of how "normal" their feelings really are.

* INDIVIDUAL GRIEF COUNSELING involves meeting one-on-one with a psychotherapist or trained religious counselor. It allows you to focus completely on your own concerns and problems. This is also a good way to gain reassurance about how normal your feelings are and has the added advantage of providing a more in-depth and personal approach to your needs.

CHAPTER FOURTEEN

Home Alone

"I dread that moment when I walk in the door after being away and I realize my wife isn't there anymore."

While it's often comforting to come back to the familiarity of the surroundings you shared with your spouse, it's also painful. There are times, such as when you return from a trip, when you're painfully reminded of who isn't there but should be. For some, the very lack of a spouse's presence, his or her voice, or habits create a sort of silence that can, at times, feel unbearable.

Being alone in your home may also make you more anxious about safety. Many people have told us that even in instances where their spouses were at home sick and helpless, there was an illusion of being protected.

TO STAY OR NOT TO STAY

"My children are urging me to sell my home and move near them. They don't seem to understand how comforting it is for me to be around all the things that hold cherished memories."

Sometimes well-meaning family members become concerned about your ability to manage alone and urge you to move. Unless it is a problem, such as your inability to care for yourself, it's usually best to stay put at least for the first year. Your home is a connection to your lost spouse, and the familiarity of the setting, the routines, and the people around you provide an important source of stability when life can seem pretty shaky. For more about handling family pressure, see Chapter 17, **Where's The Fire?**

COPING

If you are staying put and can care for yourself, how do you deal with the silence and concerns about safety? Here are some approaches we have found helpful:

- **LEAVE A T.V. OR RADIO ON WHILE YOU'RE IN THE HOUSE.**
  The sound of human voices can be comforting.

- **CALL FRIENDS AND FAMILY.**
  Being reminded you're not completely alone in the world is reassuring. Your telephone can provide a way of feeling connected to the rest of the world.

- **CONSIDER RENTING OUT A SPARE ROOM.**
  Inquire at your church or synagogue. A WORD OF CAUTION: be certain to get references for anyone who may wish to rent your room.

- **GET A PET.**
  It's true what they say about the companionship of a pet. Dogs can also provide a sense of being protected.

- **ARRANGE FOR A FRIEND OR FRIENDS TO CALL OR DROP BY AT A REGULAR TIME EVERY DAY.**

This "check-in" can be as brief as you wish and on a temporary basis. The first few months after a loss, a daily call is very reassuring.

- **INSTALL EXTRA LOCKS OR OTHER SAFETY DEVICES AROUND YOUR HOME.**

Some local police departments will send out an officer to help you evaluate safety needs. Find out if there's a Neighborhood Watch program in your area, and get to know your neighbors better.

- **THINK AHEAD ABOUT ANY SORT OF EMERGENCY AND PLAN TO HAVE SOMEONE YOU CAN CONTACT FOR ASSISTANCE.**

This can include anything from severe weather conditions to a medical problem requiring a doctor's care. If there's a chance that weather might cause telephone lines to be out of order, discuss with your neighbors a way to signal them in case you should need help. If you're concerned about situations where you might need medical assistance, check your local phone book for life or medic alert systems that can be hooked up to your telephone.

CHAPTER FIFTEEN

Back To Work

Returning to a job after a spouse's death is a step that tends to be anticipated with eagerness, dread, or both, at different times. The workplace can seem like a familiar well-ordered refuge where you find many hours of distraction away from your pain. On the other hand, it can represent the ordeal of work pressures, coworkers' reactions, and a boss's unrealistic expectations.

HOW TO MAKE IT THROUGH A WORK DAY WHILE YOU'RE GRIEVING

- WHILE YOUR PRIVATE WORLD HAS BEEN DRASTICALLY CHANGED, YOUR WORKPLACE HAS GONE ALONG IN ITS USUAL WAY. You may, therefore, initially feel out of sync with the rest of your coworkers.

- COWORKERS WILL LOOK TO YOU FOR THEIR CUE. As we discuss in Chapter 16, **Other People's Reactions,** others usually feel awkward about expressing feelings or knowing the "right thing" to say. How you respond to the first expressions of sympathy will convey a message to other coworkers about how and if you want to deal with the loss.

Some possible responses include: "Thank you. It's difficult to talk right now. Maybe later," or "I appreciate your concern." Remember the choice is yours.

- SOME COWORKERS MAY NOT MENTION THE LOSS. This can feel hurtful and even insulting. Try to bear in mind that people are often afraid of "reminding" or "upsetting" a grieving person. Expressing sadness can seem especially threatening in a work setting, where personal distress is suppossed to take a back seat to the demands of business.

- BE PREPARED FOR UNEXPECTED TEARS. During the first week back at work, there may be moments you find yourself tearful. This will get better with time, but for now, give yourself permission to retreat to the restroom or another secluded area for a good cry or to compose yourself. Many find giving themselves this "release" helps relieve the pressure of having to control feelings of grief while at work.

- BE PREPARED TO EXPERIENCE SOME DIFFICULTY WITH MEMORY AND CONCENTRATION. Remember, these are common but *temporary* symptoms of grief. While you may feel frustrated and anxious about this change, try to be patient with yourself. It helps to reread and/or go over information or tasks more than once.

- YOUR BOSS OR COWORKERS MAY HAVE UNREALISTIC EXPECTATIONS. Assure them you're doing your best, and that any slowdown on your part is temporary. If necessary, have them read portions of this book.

- DESPITE HOW OTHER'S MAY REACT, IT IS IMPORTANT FOR YOU TO RECOGNIZE THAT WHAT IS GOING ON IS NORMAL AND TEMPORARY. With time and patience (especially your own), you will regain the capacity you used to have to do your job.

CHAPTER SIXTEEN

Other People's Reactions

WHEN OTHERS "PUT THEIR FOOT IN THEIR MOUTHS"

Most well-meaning people approach a condolence situation with a mixture of anxiety and awkwardness. This sometimes results in their blurting out remarks that come across as insensitive or presumptuous. Here are some of our favorites:

"It's all for the best."

"Well, at least he/she lived a good/long life."

"I know exactly how you feel."

"He/she wouldn't want you to be sad. You have to try and be strong for: (him, her, the children, your in-laws, the family dog).

"Aren't you over it yet?"

"Don't worry. You'll find someone else."

"I went through the same thing during my divorce."

WHY OTHERS MAY ACT DIFFERENTLY TOWARDS YOU

Your loss is going to stir up many feelings in those around you. These reactions may be confusing, irritating, or even hurtful. Try to keep in mind that other people's responses are about *them*. Chances are underneath whatever they're saying or doing is probably anxiety, due to one or more of the following:

* A SENSE OF THEIR OWN HELPLESSNESS. Many people don't know what to say or do when someone they know has suffered a loss. In an attempt to overcome their sense of helplessness, they may chatter away, talk around it, or treat you like a child. People who have gone through a divorce may relate their own experiences, not realizing that death is final in a way that divorce is not.

* DIFFICULTY WITH LOSS ITSELF. Some people want to believe grief doesn't last long and that once you've had a few bad days, everything is OK and back to normal. They may say things like "Aren't you over his/her death yet?" or "You just have to get on with your life;" or "Don't dwell on the sadness; try to remember the happy times".

* FEAR THAT SOMEONE THEY DEPEND ON WON'T BE ABLE TO TAKE CARE OF THEM ANYMORE. This concern is a common source of anxiety for children, teenagers and adult children. They tend to have unrealistic expectations about the amount of time bereavement takes.

SINCE YOU ASKED

It may be hard to respond when others ask, "So how are you doing?" You might feel pressure to downplay how you're really feeling. This is probably due to a fear of upsetting either yourself or the other person. Pretending you're "doing just fine" can make you resentful, yet it may be the only way to avoid going into painful detail.

Here are some tried and true replies that are both brief and honestly reflect how you feel:

> *"I have my good days and bad days."*
>
> *"I'm doing as well as can be expected under the circumstances."*
>
> *"I'm trying to take things one day at a time."*

"OH, I DIDN'T KNOW!"

Chances are that at some point, maybe on the street, in the market, or at a social gathering, you'll encounter someone who hasn't yet heard of your loss. In those acutely uncomfortable moments following their question, "So how is your wife/husband?" the pain of the loss and/or the events around it is again stirred up for you. You struggle to reply and then have to deal with the other person's shock and embarrassment, making you feel as though you now have to take care of them.

Often people feel uncertain about how detailed an explanation to give. Keep it as simple as you wish. A possible response to the above query might be:

> *"This has really caught us both off guard. Briefly, here is what happened ... "*

COUPLE FRIENDS

When you've been part of a couple for a long time, it can take time before you really feel like a "single" person. As you try to adjust to this profound change, you may also find yourself faced with changes in how your couple friends react to you. Some couples will maintain their relationships with you; others might feel threatened and start avoiding you. This can feel very hurtful; and, in fact, add to the sense of abandonment you're already experiencing. When couple friends back away:

* It's usually because (through no fault of yours) you remind them that all relationships eventually end, as will theirs.

* They're anxious about having a formerly "safe" (i.e., married) friend now become "available". While dating of any kind may be the farthest thing from your mind, couples who are insecure about themselves can become easily threatened by any friend who is single.

Many who encounter this discomfort with couple friends gradually pull away from these relationships and begin to develop new friendships with other single people. While you may feel reluctant to make this change, you'll be gaining the support and companionship of others like yourself. For more on this important transition, see Chapter 21, **Shifting Gears.**

There are situations where women (and often men) report being sexually approached by a friend or associate of their spouse. This generally feels like both a betrayal and a violation of your trust.

There are a variety of ways to handle unwanted sexual advances (whether verbal and/or physical). Use the approach that feels right for you. Here are two suggested responses:

1. "You've obviously misread me/the situation. I'm not interested."

or

2. "Let me be absolutely clear about this. I have no intention of becoming (sexually) involved with you. Don't ever say/do that again."

CHAPTER SEVENTEEN

Where's The Fire?

In the weeks and months following the death of your spouse, well-meaning friends and relatives may begin to push you to make important decisions (from clearing out closets to selling your home) at a time when emotional upheaval has left you least able to use your best judgment.

In some cases, your family, or even you, may feel the urge to move out of your home because of "too many painful reminders." In our experience, moving away too quickly after a spouse's death may have serious emotional consequences. While it's sometimes necessary for everyone to avoid certain reminders, trying to get away from all of them doesn't lessen grief. It only postpones it. Leaving behind what's familiar and putting yourself into a new and different setting could just add to your anxiety (more adjustments), as well as your sense of loss while you mourn the people and things left behind.

So, if the heat is on to make those big decisions, here are some good rules of thumb:

- ▶ TRUST YOUR OWN INSTINCTS WHILE SORTING OUT WELL-MEANING ADVICE FROM

OTHERS. *You are the world's best expert on you.* You'll know when the time has come to take action.

- ▶ PUSHING YOURSELF TO DO SOMETHING BEFORE YOU FEEL READY CAN OFTEN RESULT IN LATER REGRETS.

- ▶ UNLESS YOU HAVE NO CHOICE, TRY NOT TO MAKE ANY MAJOR DECISIONS DURING THE FIRST YEAR FOLLOWING YOUR SPOUSE'S DEATH.

WHAT TO TAKE YOUR TIME WITH

Clearing out closets and/or giving away your spouse's possessions. Trust yourself to know when you're ready to let go of your loved one's possessions. *Take your time* deciding what's precious to you and important to keep. Should your feelings change once it's been given away, it will be too late to retrieve.

- ▶ VISITING THE BURIAL SITE. Unless you find this comforting, take as long as you need. It takes time before some people feel ready to visit the cemetery or location of their spouse's remains.

- ▶ SELLING THE CAR OR HOME. You need the comfort of familiar things associated with your spouse. Unless there's a pressing reason, hold off taking this step until at least a year has passed.

- ▶ MAJOR FINANCIAL DECISIONS. Again, give yourself time to return to your normal reasoning abilities. If a delay makes you anxious, consult a trusted financial specialist about the consequences of postponing any decisions.

- MOVING TO ANOTHER CITY OR STATE. As we've just discussed, leaving familiar surroundings too quickly can leave you feeling more stressed, anxious and isolated.

- SOCIALIZING. Sometimes friends and family urge us to "get out there and meet someone." For help in handling different aspects of the dating question, refer to Chapter 11, **You're Young and Lost Your Partner** and Chapter 22, **Am I Really Ready For This?** If you're simply feeling lonely and a little isolated, try to seek out group activities like classes, church groups, or volunteer work. That way, you can just be around people or even make new friends, depending on what seems right for you at the time.

Chapter Eighteen

Surviving Holidays and Other Special Occasions

The first year is just that: the first birthday, anniversary, holidays, etc., without your spouse. You may face special occasions that mark a milestone in your children's lives, such as graduations or weddings. Like most recently widowed, the prospect of getting through these special days probably fills you with anxiety and apprehension. At such times, the pain of loss is sharply felt, as it is triggered by:

* Having to face the occasion without your spouse

* Engaging in activities or rituals you used to share with your spouse.

* Feeling deprived of the joy of sharing the occasion with your spouse.

It's not uncommon to deny the emotional impact of these events by referring to them as "just another day." No matter what you tell yourself, however, chances are, sooner or later, you will have a reaction. The more you try to avoid dealing with loss, the greater the possibility is of a sneak attack of emotions, often when you're least ready for them.

The best way to cope with these occasions is to follow the "Scout's Rule": *always be prepared.*

THINK AHEAD. Try to anticipate how you may react and think about what will make it easiest to get through the day. Treat yourself gently.

DON'T KEEP YOURSELF ISOLATED. Plan some time during the day to be with other people, even if it's only meeting a friend for coffee or lunch.

MAKE TIME TO GRIEVE. Either on the day itself or some time before, set aside some moments to think about and feel the loss. Focusing on the sadness in this way helps "relieve the pressure" and, if needed, creates a safe time and place for tears.

KEEP YOUR EXPECTATIONS REALISTIC. You are recovering from a great loss and may not be feeling like your usual festive self. Just because you usually do things in a certain way, doesn't mean that this year can't be an exception. Others will understand.

ELIMINATE OR MINIMIZE EMOTIONALLY STRESSFUL SITUATIONS. You have choices about which activities and/or rituals you want to keep. Many people find it's easier the first year after the death to modify how they celebrate special occasions. You may, for example, want to ask a friend or relative to help you with preparations like gift buying or cooking.

REMEMBER THAT WITH TIME THE PAIN YOU FEEL ON THESE OCCASIONS WILL SOFTEN. For now, give yourself permission to do what feels right for you on these special days.

THE IMPORTANT THING IS TO "GET THROUGH" THE DAY AS BEST YOU CAN. Sometimes the anticipation of the day ahead is worse than the actual event.

HOLIDAY GET-TOGETHERS

Even when you've prepared yourself by making time to grieve beforehand, you may feel anxious about becoming uncomfortable in a festive gathering. There's often a sense of being "out of it," as you watch others having a good time.

However, just *going*, even if you need to leave early, is a sign of progress. It can also help you gain a sense of control in these situations by:

GIVING YOURSELF THE FIRST 30 MINUTES AFTER YOU ARRIVE TO ADJUST TO THE SITUATION. Remember this is a new situation (without your spouse). Expect some uneasiness for a short time. Many people discover that once they've made it past the first half hour, they begin to feel more relaxed.

CONTACTING THE HOST OR HOSTESS AHEAD OF TIME AND MAKING THEM AWARE THAT YOU AREN'T YOUR USUAL SELF AND MAY FEEL THE NEED TO LEAVE EARLY.

TAKING YOUR OWN CAR OR ALERTING A FRIEND WHO'S DRIVING THAT YOU MAY WANT TO LEAVE EARLY.

TAKING A TIME-OUT IF YOU'RE FEELING OVERWHELMED, SO YOU CAN RETREAT TO A PRIVATE PLACE (LIKE A BATHROOM OR BEDROOM) OR TAKE A WALK, FOR A BRIEF CRY. Most people will understand your need to do this.

BREAKING THE ICE

At family gatherings, everyone will be aware of your loss. They may feel awkward about making any mention of it out of fear of "upsetting you." In fact, you may actually feel more hurt and upset if everyone is avoiding the subject. In addition to which, not talking about the person everyone is thinking about only creates a sense of tension at a gathering.

Others will take their cue from you. It's helpful, therefore, at a point that is comfortable for you, to mention your spouse in whatever way you wish. You might, for example, bring up the name as part of a toast or prayer at dinner. Even casual comments, such as: "Gee, Henry always loved Aunt Edna's mince pie," or "Remember how Judy used to get a kick out of decorating for the holidays?", are effective ice breakers.

CHAPTER NINETEEN

Making Money Matters More Manageable

"There's a mountain of bills on my dining room table that just keeps getting bigger by the week: mortgage payments, utility bills, car insurance, legal and accounting services, funeral expenses. As though that weren't enough, I keep getting bills from the hospital, doctors and even the ambulance company. I feel so overwhelmed, I just avoid dealing with any of it."

The prospect of facing financial concerns when you're already stressed by bereavement can seem unbearable. In addition to the usual expenses of life, you are now confronted by the financial consequences of illness and death. Many people experience some anxiety, anger, and even panic when medical or funeral-related bills arrive because:

- They're a reminder of the painful events surrounding the loss of your spouse.

- They're a further expense and/or hassle at a time when you feel already emotionally and perhaps economically drained.

- You may have to make numerous and/or difficult phone calls to clear up confusing or incorrect billing situations. Dealing with bureaucratic red tape is a headache even in the best of times.

DEALING WITH THE SITUATION

OVERWHELMED? ASK A TRUSTED FRIEND OR RELATIVE TO HELP. They might sort through mail, make phone calls or help you determine what needs immediate attention.

WHEN ORDERING DEATH CERTIFICATES FROM THE COUNTY HALL OF RECORDS, BE SURE TO ORDER AT LEAST FIVE AND AS MANY AS TEN OR MORE COPIES. You may need more, depending on your financial situation. The Social Security Administration, insurance companies, and financial institutions require a certified copy of the death certificate.

ADDITIONAL COPIES WILL ALSO BE NEEDED TO CHANGE THE OWNERSHIP OF YOUR HOME OR CAR TO YOUR OWN NAME.

EVEN IF YOU HAVE MEDICAL INSURANCE, HOSPITALS, DOCTORS, AND AMBULANCE COMPANIES MAY BILL YOU INDEPENDENTLY. Don't panic. Call your health insurer and get help in clearing up any confusion.

IF YOU DON'T HAVE MEDICAL INSURANCE, AND YOU'RE OVERWHELMED BY MEDICAL

EXPENSES, DON'T PANIC. Contact the various billing offices, explain your situation, and be prepared to suggest a payment arrangement.

BE AWARE THAT IF YOUR CREDIT WAS IN YOUR SPOUSE'S NAME, IT MAY BE DIFFICULT TO ESTABLISH CREDIT ON YOUR OWN. If asked, you should be honest about your current status.

CONSULT YOUR ACCOUNTANT OR ATTORNEY.

► A WORD OF CAUTION HERE: Some people who offer "helpful" suggestions may actually be acting out of self-interest. Get advice only from people you know and can trust or who come recommended by close friends. There are very charming, persuasive con artists who prey on the recently bereaved.

KEEPING YOUR HEAD ABOVE WATER

At some point, you'll probably need to ask yourself one or more of the following questions:

- Can I make ends meet on my present income?
- How long will it take to pay off debts?
- Will I have to find a job or change my present employment situation to earn more income?
- Will I need more training or schooling to make myself more marketable in today's world?

REMEMBER: The first few months are the most difficult, so don't rush into anything. Try to postpone any major decisions about finances or employment for as long as possible.

Consult with your local social security office or accountant about social security benefits for yourself or your children. Also check with your spouse's former employer about pension plan benefits.

FAMILY HASSLES OVER INHERITANCE

Any conflicts that existed in your family before your spouse died will probably come up at some point after the death. Sometimes the death itself will add more fuel to the fire. This is especially so where there are rivalries between family members. With a death, this rivalry usually focuses on whatever inheritance (money and/or possessions) may exist. You've probably heard or read about families where inheritance battles turned especially nasty.

Conflicts over who gets what and who's feeling cheated are often really about how loved or favored each person felt. Possessions and money represent love and/or recognition in many relationships, so not being left something can feel to the survivor like a painful message of rejection.

While your family's bickering may not have reached that point, it can still be especially difficult to deal with any conflicts when you're feeling so emotionally drained by grief. Here are some ways to handle stormy family situations:

For now, it's important to protect yourself as much as possible from additional stress. Give yourself permission to step out of any conflicts that require major decisions at this time. You might say to your family:

> *"Right now I'm not feeling up to dealing with this. Let's agree to make some time in the future to get together and discuss it."*

ACKNOWLEDGE WITH YOUR FAMILY THAT, AT SOME POINT, THESE CONFLICTS WILL BE TACKLED WITH A NEUTRAL REFEREE, EITHER IN A FAMILY CONFERENCE OR FAMILY COUNSELING. Consider utilizing a professional mediator who specializes in legal issues, an attorney, a mental health professional, or a clergyman trained in dispute mediation.

CHAPTER TWENTY

Postal Predicaments

RECEIVING MAIL

You've probably already been confronted with one or both of these painful situations: bills, advertisements, or even holiday cards arrive in the mail addressed to your spouse. Or you happen to be somewhere and bump into someone who hasn't heard of the death (see Chapter 16, **Other People's Reactions.**)

Expect to experience some reaction to these situations. Unfortunately, there's little you can do to guard against such painful reminders of your loss.

GETTING THE WORD OUT

Notifying family, friends, and business associates of the death is usually a matter of word of mouth, either in person, by telephone, or through an obituary notice.

People you correspond with infrequently may be sent a form letter as a way of explaining what has happened. Or you might prefer to put off writing until first hearing from the other person(s).

Here's an example of what could be written in a note. Use only the parts that seem right for you:

> Dear Friends,
>
> This is very difficult to have to tell you.
>
> We've recently experienced a loss in our family. On (date death occured), (name of your spouse) died (suddenly or after an illness). (BRIEF description of the circumstances and cause of death.)
>
> I'd really appreciate hearing from you sometime soon.
>
> Sincerely,

WRITING THANK-YOU NOTES

Many people procrastinate when it comes to responding to sympathy cards or flowers. If you feel up to sending a brief note or making a quick phone call, do so. If not, don't worry about it. Most people understand and don't expect a reply given the circumstances, but it will help to keep in touch if they hear from you.

Part Three

Moving On

CHAPTER TWENTY-ONE

Shifting Gears

NO LONGER A COUPLE

One of the most difficult changes that comes with losing a spouse is the loss of your identity as part of *a couple*. In general, the longer you were married or the younger you were at the time of marriage, the more your sense of yourself is likely to have blended with your spouse. Many couples have "grown up" together.

It may seem difficult to remember a time before your spouse was in your life, so to now be labeled "single" by others can feel jarring. *Give yourself time*. It usually takes awhile to become accustomed to feeling "not married."

As you struggle to adjust to a sense of yourself without a partner, you may discover uncomfortable feelings surfacing when you're around people who still have partners.

> *"Why is my spouse gone, and they still have theirs?"*

You may feel somewhat guilty about the envy you experience in these situations. It's normal and very understandable.

"Look at that couple argue! Don't they realize how short life is? They should appreciate every second they have together. If only ..."

Many people also become angry and resentful when the pain of their loss is stirred up by seeing other couples' fighting or bickering over what seem to be petty problems.

FINDING NEW FRIENDS

The need for companionship is natural. Sometimes a spouse was the primary person with whom you did things. Now that you are without him or her, you may feel isolated and lonely.

Look around you. Do you already have friends, neighbors, or acquaintances who are on their own and available to join you in doing things? If not, or if you'd like to enlarge your current circle of friends, here are some suggestions:

- CONTACT YOUR LOCAL CHAMBER OF COMMERCE. Ask for a list by mail of special interest clubs and organizations in your community.

- VOLUNTEER WORK. Check out opportunies through local newspapers or volunteer agencies or contact specific service groups that interest you.

- CHURCH GROUPS OR CLASSES. Most churches and synagogues offer a variety of activities.

- CLASSES AT LOCAL ADULT SCHOOLS OR COMMUNITY COLLEGES.

- LOCAL POLITICAL ORGANIZATIONS. There's generally something for everyone to do, even if it's stuffing envelopes.

- WIDOWED AND BEREAVEMENT SUPPORT GROUPS. (See Chapter 13, **People Do Need People.**)

► A WORD OF CAUTION: You're especially vulnerable right now. As you meet new people, be careful of those who may prey on the recently widowed.

Chapter Twenty-Two

Am I Really Ready For This?

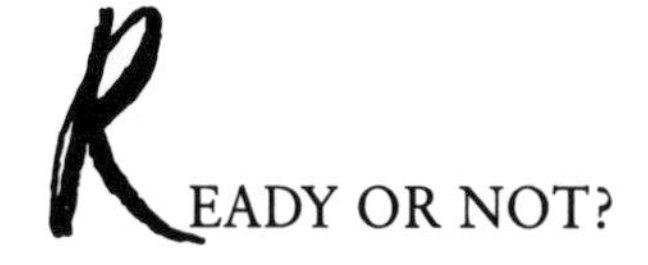

EADY OR NOT?

You may not want to even consider the idea of dating.

You may feel ready to think about the possibility.

You may be at a point where you are ready to try dating.

One of the final stages of the bereavement process is where you begin to seriously consider the possibility of forming new attachments. This may mean creating friendships with members of the same sex or opposite sex (see Chapter 21, **Shifting Gears**). Or it may indicate a wish to explore a romantic and/or sexual relationship. This doesn't mean you want to *forget* your spouse, but rather it reflects a growing readiness for the companionship and intimacy you once shared with someone.

LISTENING TO YOURSELF

Friends and family will often drop hints or make suggestions about "fixing you up" or going to "singles" activities. It's important not to let others pressure you. Trust your own feelings and sense of when the time is right.

Even if you do feel ready to test the waters of the singles' scene, don't be surprised if at first you find yourself experiencing some of these feelings:

GUILT. It's not uncommon to feel *survivor guilt* as you reach this stage. Because you want to begin enjoying life once again, it may feel as though you're being disloyal to and/or leaving behind your dead spouse. If feelings of guilt persist, it could be a sign that you have more grieving to do.

ANGER. You may find yourself angry at your spouse: "If you hadn't died, I wouldn't have to go through this."

ANXIETY. Of course you're anxious! After all, when was the last time you were single?

WHAT'S DIFFERENT NOW

How old were you when you last dated? What were the dating customs and rules then? Many people report that when they first reenter the singles' world, they feel like Rip Van Winkle: on the inside it's as though they were still the age they were when last single. On the outside though, the world has changed. Some of the biggest changes you'll probably discover include:

WOMEN MAKING THE FIRST MOVE. It's now not uncommon for a woman to initiate a phone call, invite a man to an event such as a concert or movie, or suggest dinner at her place at some time.

WOMEN PAYING FOR THEMSELVES. In some cases, a woman may view paying her own way as freeing her from any "obligation" to the man. Or it may just be a case of economics: if both people live on fixed incomes, it's more thrifty to share the expense of a night out.

SEXUAL CONDUCT. Even in this time of increased caution, many people engage in sex sooner than they once did.

REMEMBER: Regardless of what others are doing, *you are the best judge of what is right for you*. Keep in mind, however, that if you were a teenager when you last dated, you probably followed your parents' guidelines about what was permissible. Now that you are an adult, you're able to make choices about what is right for you.

GETTING YOUR FEET WET

OK, you're ready to start easing your way into the social life of a single person. How exactly should you go about it?

Your attitude in approaching this step is important. Try to think in terms of a shopping experience. You'll want to "try on" the different ways and places to meet someone until you find a good "fit". In the process, you'll get a chance to learn what doesn't fit or appeal to you. With that philosophy in mind:

IF YOU'RE COMFORTABLE WITH IT, LET FRIENDS AND FAMILY KNOW YOU'RE READY TO MEET NEW PEOPLE.

FIND A FRIEND WHO IS CURRENTLY SINGLE

Ask your friend for advice about the current rules and customs. But remember: no matter how well-meaning advice can be, *you* always need to adapt it to what feels right for *you*.

CHECK OUT CHURCH-RELATED SOCIAL ACTIVITIES.

CHECK LOCAL PAPERS FOR SINGLES' ACTIVITIES. Many people feel more relaxed when there's an activity such as hiking, bridge, theater, gourmet cooking, etc., to focus on rather than just "meeting someone." If you are over fifty-five, consider joining Elderhostel, an organization that combines travel with learning in a way that's comfortable for people on their own.

BRING A FRIEND ALONG THE FIRST TIME YOU TRY ANYTHING NEW. It's a good idea to discuss before you go what each of you will do in the event one of you meets someone, wants to leave early, or is uncomfortable.

TAKING THE PLUNGE INTO DATING

Trust yourself to know when it's time to start dating. That doesn't mean you won't be anxious or uncertain. Some anxiety on any date is natural and, in your situation, expected. Don't try to bluff it out. What often helps is to let the other person know you are new at this.

One of the most important things to remember in starting any new relationship is that a new person is a new learning experience. You had years to get to know your spouse and adjust to the ways you reacted to each other. A new person can't be expected to react in the same ways as your spouse did. It takes time to know each other.

► A WORD OF WARNING: Sometimes people jump into dating to erase the pain they're feeling. They hope the excitement of a new relationship will make the pain go away. Dating for that reason can backfire. You aren't being fair to a new relationship when you haven't taken enough time to emotionally finish with the old one.

READY OR NOT FOR SEX?

It's natural to feel considerable anxiety about engaging in sex. Feelings of guilt about your dead spouse may start to crop up and get in the way. Or there may have been reasons why you and your spouse weren't sexually active for awhile. Or some of you may be wrestling with issues of morality. All of these can cause anxiety.

KEEP THE FOLLOWING POINTS IN MIND:

IF YOU FEEL REALLY ANXIOUS, YOU MAY JUST NEED MORE TIME. Give yourself permission to move at a pace that's right for you.

REMIND YOURSELF THAT EACH NEW PERSON IS A LEARNING PROCESS. You and your spouse had years to work out what was right for both of you. No two people react the same way sexually or otherwise.

THE KEYS TO A GOOD SEXUAL RELATIONSHIP ARE TRUST AND COMMUNICATION. It's important to feel free to tell each other what you are and are not comfortable with.

Part Four

Help Along The Way

Chapter Twenty-Three

Clip This Chapter and Carry It With You

If it's one of those times when coping with your loss feels especially difficult, consider:

- ▶ **IT DOES GET BETTER.**
- ▶ **EVERY TEAR HELPS.** The best way to get through grieving is to do the grieving.
- ▶ **YOU WILL GRIEVE IN YOUR OWN WAY AND IN YOUR OWN TIME.**
- ▶ **FOR NOW, NOT NORMAL IS NORMAL.**
- ▶ **YOUR WHOLE WORLD HAS BEEN TURNED UPSIDE DOWN.** Be *gentle* with yourself.
- ▶ **YOUR LIMITATIONS IN COPING ARE TEMPORARY.** With time, you'll get better at handling new responsibilities.
- ▶ **TRUST YOUR OWN INSTINCTS WHILE SORTING OUT WELL-MEANING ADVICE FROM OTHERS.** You are the world's *best* expert on *you*.

- **TRY NOT TO LET OTHERS PRESSURE YOU.** What is right for someone else is not necessarily right for *you*.

- **IF POSSIBLE, POSTPONE ANY MAJOR DECISIONS FOR THE FIRST YEAR.** Your ability to make sound judgements is *temporarily out of order*.

- **BE PATIENT WITH YOURSELF.** Don't expect to be able to make serious plans at a time when having to decide what to do *tomorrow* can feel overwhelming.

- **FOR NOW, IT'S OK TO ASK FOR HELP FROM OTHERS.** Nobody's strong all the time. Even Superman can be weakened by Kryptonite.

- **CONFUSION AND MEMORY LOSS ARE NORMAL AND TEMPORARY SYMPTOMS.**

- **THE FIRST YEAR IS FULL OF FIRST EVERYTHINGS.**

- **ANY NEW SITUATION WILL START OUT BEING UNCOMFORTABLE THE FIRST TIME.** The next time is always easier.

Bereavement is a *learning experience* about *you*. You will discover new capabilities and strengths you didn't realize you had.

GOOD LUCK!

CHAPTER TWENTY-FOUR

Resources For Help Along The Way

EMOTIONAL HELP

SUICIDE

If you feel that you might hurt yourself, call your local operator who will immediately connect you with the Suicide Hot Line in your area.

For families who have survived suicide, call:

> **AMERICAN ASSOCIATION OF SUICIDOLOGY; 1-202-237-2280**, for informaton about support groups, journals, and books written by survivors and specialists.

INDIVIDUAL/FAMILY COUNSELING

To locate a mental health professional, contact your local mental health clinic or hospital or the local chapters of the following organizations (here are national numbers in case you can't find chapters in your area):

> **AMERICAN PSYCHIATRIC ASSOCIATION; 1-202-682-6000.** Referral to your local chapter. Remember that psychiatrists specialize in prescribing medications for emotional concerns in addition to providing psychotherapy.

AMERICAN BOARD OF EXAMINERS IN CLINICAL SOCIAL WORK,
1-800-694-5285, or e-mail abecsw.org. Referral to your local chapter will put you in touch with an experienced, licensed clinical social worker for individual or family grief counseling. Be sure to request a therapist who specializes in bereavement.

AMERICAN PSYCHOLOGICAL ASSOCIATION,
1-202-336-5500. Will refer you to your local chapter. Request a psychologist who specializes in bereavement.

NATIONAL ASSOCIATION OF SOCIAL WORKERS,
1-800-638-8799. Ask for the number of the NASW Referral Service in your area.

SUPPORT GROUPS

Contact hospitals, hospices, churches, synagogues, or mental health clinics in your area. Or try:

AMERICAN ASSOCIATION OF RETIRED PEOPLE (AARP),
601 E Street, N.W., Washington, DC 20049; 1-800-424-3410. AARP has a Widowed Persons Service Program that sponsors local support groups.

PARENTS WITHOUT PARTNERS (POP);
1-800-637-7974. Referral to local POP programs that provide emotional support for single parents. POP also offers social activities.

GROUPS FOR CHILDREN AND ADOLESCENTS

THE DOUGY CENTER—THE NATIONAL CENTER FOR GRIEVING CHILDREN AND FAMILIES,
3909 S.E. 52nd Ave., P.O. Box 86852, Portland, Oregon 97286; 1-503-775-5683. A nationwide organization that publishes a listing of support groups for children and adolescents in your area.

TEEN GRIEF, INC.,
P.O. Box 220034, Newhall, California 91322; 1-805-253-1932. Referral to local support groups for adolescents. Also works with school counselors to set up programs to help teens cope with loss.

GENERAL INFORMATION ON COPING WITH THE LOSS OF A SPOUSE

AMERICAN ASSOCIATION OF RETIRED PERSONS,
601 E Street, N.W., Washington, DC 20049; 1-800-424-3410. Excellent source of information. Provides booklets on a variety of issues.

THE CENTERING CORPORATION,
1531 N. Saddle Creek Road, Omaha, Nebraska 68104-5064; 1-402-553-1200. Will send inspirational newsletter, *Caring Concepts,* upon request.

Also has bereavement book service that provides free catalogues.

Please note that while the following Web sites are current as of the publication of this edition, there may be changes over time. We suggest you check for updated information under the categories of *Widowed*, *Widower*, and *Young Widowed.*

Two current Web sites that offer extensive information on resources such as support groups, books, and interactive forums include:

GriefNet
Web site: www.rivendell.org

WidowNet
Web site: www.fortnet.org/widownet

LEGAL/FINANCIAL ASSISTANCE

THE BAR ASSOCIATION. Contact your local chapter for a referral to an attorney in your area who specializes in dealing with your specific concerns.

AMERICAN COLLEGE OF TRUST AND ESTATE COUNSEL,
3415 S. Sepulveda Blvd., Suite 330, Los Angeles, California 90034; 1-310-398-1888. Will provide a list of probate attorneys who are members of their organization.

SOCIAL SECURITY ADMINISTRATION;
1-800-772-1213.
Provides information and a guide to benefits due you or your children under the age of eighteen.

VETERANS ADMINISTRATION. If your spouse was in the armed services, contact your local or state office about possible benefits due you or your child.

REENTERING THE JOB MARKET

Universities and community colleges generally offer evening and/or extension classes. Financial aid is often available.

STATE EMPLOYMENT OFFICE. Your local office provides job listings at no charge.

DISPLACED HOMEMAKERS NETWORK, 1010 VERMONT AVE., N.W. WASHINGTON, D.C. 20005; 1-202-336-5500. Offers free information about reentering the job market and will also refer you to the nearest career counseling center.

VOLUNTEER OPPORTUNITIES

Contact your local:

- Schools for foster grandparenting or tutoring
- Libraries
- Hospitals or hospices
- Meals On Wheels
- Retired Senior Volunteer Program (R.S.V.P.)
- Museums that will train docents
- Family service agencies that will train volunteers for a variety of tasks
- Local churches or synagogues

SUGGESTED READING

SUGGESTED READING

FINANCES

Martin, Renee and Martin, Don. *The Survival Guide for Women*, Washington, D.C.: Regnery Gateway. 1991.

Brown, Judith N. and Baldwin, Christina. *A Second Start: A Widow's Guide to Financial Survival at a Time of Emotional Stress*, New York, NY: Simon and Schuster. 1986.

RELATIONSHIPS

Robertson, John. *Suddenly Single*, New York, NY: Simon and Schuster. 1986.

Butler, Robert N. and Lewis, Myrna I. *Love and Sex After Forty: A Guide for Men and Women For Their Mid and Later Years*, New York, NY: Harper & Row. 1986.

HELPING CHILDREN AND ADOLESCENTS COPE

PRESCHOOL CHILDREN

Prestine, Joan Singleton. *Someone Special Died.* Price/Stein/Sloan, New York, NY: 1987.

Stein, Sarah Barnet. *About Dying*, New York, NY: Walker and Company. 1974.

Viorst, Judith. *The Tenth Good Thing About Barney*, New York, NY: Atheneum. 1972.

YOUNG SCHOOL-AGE CHILDREN

Grollman, Earl. *Talking About Death: A Dialogue Between Parent and Child*, Boston, MA: Beacon Press. 1985.

Fassler, Joan. *My Grandpa Died Today*, New York, NY: Human Sciences Press. 1971.

Hughes, Phyllis Rash. *Dying Is Different*, Mahomet, IL: Mech Mentor Educational. 1978.

OLDER SCHOOL-AGE CHILDREN

White, E.B.. *Charlotte's Web*, New York, NY: Harper & Row. 1952.

LeShaun, Eva. *Learning to Say Goodbye When a Parent Dies*, New York, NY: Avon. 1978.

ALL AGES

Krementz, Jill. *How It Feels When a Parent Dies*, New York, NY: Alfred A. Knopf. 1981.

Grollman, Earl A.. *Talking About Death*, Boston, MA: Beacon Press. 1970.

Rofes, Eric E.. *The Kid's Book About Death and Dying*, Boston, MA: Little, Brown & Co. 1985.

We Want To Hear From You

Dear Reader:

Because we continue to learn from you, we'd appreciate knowing your reactions to *LOST MY PARTNER - WHAT'LL I DO?* Your comments are important and help us ensure that we are providing the most effective guidance to those who have lost a spouse. If you need more space than is provided, please enclose this form with as many additional pages as you wish.

Now that you have read this book:

1. Which chapters and/or coping techniques were most helpful?

2. Where any chapters or suggestions uncomfortable or not helpful?

3. What should we have included that we didn't?

General Comments:

(OPTIONAL)

Name:______________________________________

Address:____________________________________

____

Telephone:(_____)____________________________

Thank you for taking time to respond.

Sincerely,
Laurie and Ruth

Please clip, fold, and mail this form to the address already printed on the back. Or fax the form to: (310) 379-1373.

Feel free to correspond with us at length. We can be reached at: McCormick Press, P.O. Box 608, Manhattan Beach, California 90267-0608. Or by e-mail at: McCorPress@aol.com.

Order Form

<u>To order the book "*Lost My Partner - What'll I Do?*"</u>

Fax orders: (310) 379-1373

Telephone orders: Call toll free: 1-877-727-3814.
Have your Discover, MasterCard or VISA ready

On-line orders: McCorPress@aol.com

Postal orders: McCormick Press
P. O. Box 608
Manhattan Beach, CA 90267-0608

No. of books __________ @ $12.95/book = ______________

Sales Tax (CA residents add 8.25%) ______________
Shipping/Handling ($4.00 for first book—
$2.00 for each additional book) ______________

Payment:

Check: Make payable to McCormick Press and mail to the above address

Credit Card: ☐ Discover ☐ MasterCard ☐ VISA

Card No.:__________________________ Exp. Date_________

Name on card:____

Ship to:
Name:____

Address:____

City/State/ZIP:_______________________________________

Phone No.:____

Fax:____

Order Form

To order the book "*Lost My Partner - What'll I Do?*"

Fax orders: (310) 379-1373

Telephone orders: Call toll free: 1-877-727-3814.
Have your Discover, MasterCard or VISA ready

On-line orders: McCorPress@aol.com

Postal orders: McCormick Press
P. O. Box 608
Manhattan Beach, CA 90267-0608

No. of books ____________ @ $12.95/book = ________________

Sales Tax (CA residents add 8.25%) ________________
Shipping/Handling ($4.00 for first book—
$2.00 for each additional book) ________________

Payment:

Check: Make payable to McCormick Press and mail to the above address

Credit Card: ☐ Discover ☐ MasterCard ☐ VISA

Card No.:______________________________ Exp. Date__________

Name on card:____

Ship to:
Name:____

Address:____

City/State/ZIP:____

Phone No.:____

Fax:____